The Exuberant Years:

A Guide for Junior High Leaders

Ginny Ward Holderness

JOHN KNOX PRESS
ATLANTA

Unless otherwise noted, Scripture quotations are from the Revised Standard Version Bible, copyright 1946, 1952, and © 1971 by the Division of Christian Education, National Council of the Churches of Christ in the U. S. A., and used by permission.

Acknowledgment is made for permission to quote from the following:
Breaking Free, © 1971 by Serendipity House, © 1972 by Lyman Coleman; *Discovery*, © 1972 by Lyman Coleman; *Groups in Action*, © 1968, 1971 by Lyman Coleman; Serendipity, © 1972 by Serendipity House. All in the Serendipity series by Lyman Coleman.
Communicating with Junior Highs, by Robert L. Browning. Copyright © 1968 by Graded Press.
Horns and Halos in Human Nature, by J. Wallace Hamilton. Copyright © 1954 by Fleming H. Revell Co.
From "A Platform for Youth Work," by Virginia L. Harbour. Reprinted from the *International Journal of Religious Education*, March, 1964 issue. Used by permission.
Values and Teaching, by Louis E. Raths, Merrill Harmin, and Sidney B. Simon. Copyright © 1966, Charles E. Merrill Publishing Co.
Reprinted by permission of Hart Publishing Company, Inc., from its copyrighted volume VALUES CLARIFICATION: A Handbook for Teachers and Students by Sidney B. Simon, Leland W. Howe and Howard Kirschenbaum.

Library of Congress Cataloging in Publication Data

Holderness, Ginny Ward, 1946–
    The exuberant years.

    Includes bibliographical references.
    1. Church work with adolescents.   2.   Christian education of adolescents.   I.   Title.
BV1475.9.H64   268'.433   75-13458
ISBN 0-8042-1225-2

Third printing 1978

Copyright © 1976 by John Knox Press
Printed in the United States of America

Contents

Foreword

Grades 7, 8, and 9. Young people aged 12, 13, and 14. What does one *do* with them? Why? How? Because she had the experience of working with junior highs herself and found in her conversations and in her consulting that she could communicate both her own knowledge and enthusiasm, Ginny Ward Holderness gradually found herself moving into writing a book—*The Exuberant Years: A Guide for Junior High Leaders.* As a director of Christian education, then a minister's wife and an educational consultant, she worked directly with junior highs, with adult leaders of junior highs. Not finding the kind of practical guide and resource that she needed herself, she produced one. It is clear, direct, to the point, easily comprehended. It focuses directly on junior highs, and begins to correct the overbalance of emphasis of the church on senior highs.

A writer is tempted to find answers to some questions before beginning a book. Are my theological and Biblical foundations clear and evident? Am I proceeding on the basis of sound educational and psychological theory? Will I be meeting the needs of adult leaders? One could spend a lifetime in getting ready, worrying about and working through those questions. Ginny was willing to run the risk of offering what she believed, and observed to be useful, making no pretense or assumption of speaking the final word. An observant person detects easily that her suggestions are informed by reliable theoretical perspectives, not stated as propositions and then "applied," but permeating the whole.

Or again, the question is asked, "How much of the 'new,' the current 'fad,' do I utilize?" Again, the author uses what is appropriate, not demanding perfection from any method or resource, willing to draw from a variety of resources and not elevate any one into the key position of offering the easy, sure-fire answer.

Values implicit in such attitudes and approaches are shared by Ginny and her former teacher, who introduces her to the public with delight. Her writing has within it the kind of intrinsic authority that arises out of experience, reflection, and commitment—and the sure knowledge that hard work is required, but is infinitely rewarding.

Sara Little
Professor of Christian Education
P.S.C.E. and U.T.S.

Preface

This book has been written for junior high leaders and for those who are considering working with junior highs. I don't know how many times individuals have called me and said: "Do you have any ideas for a junior high group?" It's such a difficult question. I want to say: "Yes, I do, if you have four or five hours to talk about it." What they want is program ideas, activities, things to do. What I want to give them is an approach. The success they are looking for won't come through a list of program materials. They will try one thing one night and another idea for three consecutive meetings. And, they will still be frustrated. In fact, many leaders spend the whole year taking stabs at various ideas. Then, when they evaluate the year, they tell you which activity works with junior highs and which does not. I have a hard time drawing conclusions from this kind of evaluation. A lot of the activities which they report as failures could have been successes, had they been part of a well-planned, purposeful program.

First, I need to define "program." I have never liked that word, for I picture speakers, lectures, something very dry and inflexible. By program, I mean the whole thing. Everything you do with junior highs all year long is your youth program. It should be planned with objectives. What would you like to see your youth do this year? In answering this question, consider such areas as worship, study, service, fellowship. Dream dreams. Lay out plans for the entire year. In fact, the ideal youth program planners would be making projections for the following year.

Planning is a very important part of the approach to junior high work. But, if I could work with every junior high leader who has asked for help, I would emphasize another essential part of the approach—building relationships. A major goal of your program should be to build relationships: (a) between the young person individually and the adult (you and other adults who work with you); (b) among the junior highs, within the group;

(c) between the youth and the church; and, closely connected with the church, (d) between the youth and God. The activities, studies, mini-courses, or whatever are considerably less important than the relationships which can be built as a result of "youth group."

I hope, as you read this book, that you will see the importance of building relationships, and the importance of detailed planning. Planning is the key to eliminating a lot of anxiety.

This book takes a positive approach. It asks you to draw on the best in you and to see the best in them, the junior highs. It suggests that you relax, be yourself, and have a good time with these youth. They really are a lot of fun.

Before we get started, there may be some debate as to what exactly is a junior high—age/grade-wise. Most commonly, it includes the seventh, eighth, and ninth grade. In many areas public schools combine sixth and seventh, so churches have followed suit. I think of twelve-, thirteen-, and fourteen-year-olds. This book can be used in connection with any break-down. You may have grades:

(1)   6–7–8–9 together
(2)   7–8–9
(3)   7–8
(4)   8–9

The mini-courses have been used with all four age groups. In fact, some of them have worked well with senior highs. So, if you know of any senior high leaders who need something extra, suggest they consider the eleven mini-courses in this book.

The Exuberant Years is a basics book. You could call it "Junior Highs 101." It is a guide for the new leader, who is encouraged to start at the beginning by developing an approach to youth work. The leader is to get to know his junior highs, evaluate his situation, develop goals and objectives, and plan with the youth. There are methods and mini-courses which offer options for the youth program, while more experienced leaders may primarily be interested in the mini-courses. However, I hope you will use the entire book in evaluating your own "approach" to youth work.

Writing a book gives me an opportunity to thank those persons who have helped me, not only in writing *The Exuberant Years,* but in the field of Christian Education. If it weren't for Bardarah McCandless, C.E. professor at Westminster College in New Wilmington, Pennsylvania, I may not be in this business. She's been more than a college professor; she is a friend. Many thanks go to Sara Little at P.S.C.E. who gave me the tools of the trade; I couldn't have had a more outstanding teacher. If I can meet with her once a year, I feel like I'm up on all the latest trends in education.

In preparing this book, there is one group of people who deserve a good deal of credit. (They really put up with a lot!) They were always willing to let me test ideas on them—the Junior High Youth Group at Pulaski Heights Presbyterian Church in Little Rock.

Rev. Bill Williamson was the sole inspiration for the mini-course on death. I deeply appreciated his contribution and his support. He and his wife Nancy were the first to encourage me in the writing of this book.

And I must acknowledge my enthusiastic brother-in-law, Rev. Haywood Holderness, who persisted: "When am I going to see this junior high book!"

Another thank-you to Anne Schmutz, who typed part of the manuscript.

The greatest thanks go to Jim and J. B. Jim is the kind of husband a writer needs. Not only was he encouraging and patient, but it's nice to have someone around who can give you the right word or phrasing when you are stumped. Our son, J. B., was three months old when I started writing, and I'm grateful for his long naps. Plus, he kept me laughing when I was discouraged with writing!

And I'm glad to have the opportunity to say to my Mom and Dad: I love you.

Section A

Preparation

1

Who You Are

YOU ARE FANTASTIC! Obviously, if you have this book in your hands, you must have some interest in junior highs. So, I repeat: YOU ARE FANTASTIC! Now, I am not implying that you've got to *be* (as in "become") fantastic. I am saying you *are* (as in "now") fantastic. If this sounds a little positive thinking-ish, maybe it should. Heaven knows there is enough negativism surrounding those who contemplate taking on the junior highs, or, for that matter, those who have the junior highs and are dreading Sunday night.

Okay, so you don't feel fantastic. Perhaps you feel inadequate . . . how about scared! What does it take to be a leader of junior highs? If the idea of "leading" turns you off, I will put the question another way:

What does it take to work with junior highs?

How do you relate to twelve, thirteen, and fourteen year olds?

You probably have the qualities within you. Maybe you just need something to build your confidence. The following is a job description submitted by a group of junior highs. This is what they wanted in a leader:

He or she should

(1) like junior highs.
(2) really want to work with and be with them.
(3) be enthusiastic.
(4) have some ideas—on what to do, programs, activities.
(5) have patience.
(6) have a sense of humor.
(7) not be boring.
(8) be organized.

Some people think that, to work with a junior high group, one should have lots of know-how in the areas of games, sports, crafts, and music;

that he should have various skills in leadership, teaching, and Biblical studies; and that he should be a gung-ho superman (good looking too, of course), who can attract kids like a rock star.

If that were true, we would end up with personality cults. The only reason for coming to church would be "Joe Wonderful." Then, when Joe Wonderful finishes his year or two, the youth group evaporates. Some of you may be in the situation of having to succeed a Joe Wonderful. Whatever you do, please don't get caught in the trap of trying to be like him, even if the kids do say "Well, last year, Joe did. . . ."

If that is your situation, this book might help you. Chapter 4 describes a planning process, in which you engage the youth in responsible participation in their program. You see, Joe Wonderful really didn't need to give the kids any responsibility. He "had what it takes" to run the whole show. This book is written on the assumption that:

A LEADER DOES NOT BUILD A YOUTH GROUP. YOUTH BUILD A YOUTH GROUP!

The junior highs who wrote the job description came up with some good characteristics. I would not hesitate to include them in a list of qualifications for prospective youth workers. Let's suppose I was going to talk with you about the possibility of working with our seventh, eighth, and ninth graders. I am going to ask you some questions. For each, consider the following responses:

——Yes, that's me.
——I'll consider that. I'm willing to work on that.
——That's a tough one for me. That's one of my downfalls.
——Forget it.

1. *Can you be YOU?*

I have started with the hardest. Being *you* means not having to play the "role" of teacher over pupil, of the authority figure—in other words, the "put-down syndrome." In school, at home, in the department store, the junior high is constantly reminded that he's "just a kid" to be taught, disciplined, controlled. The youth group is one place where he can enjoy a friendly relationship with an adult.

Being you means letting them know who you are. Be open with them. Relax. Junior highs are very conversant. They will be anxious to know your feelings and opinions.

2. *Can you listen?*

They do talk a *lot*. They long for an adult who will listen without making moral judgments. Church teachers and leaders are often overly concerned with being a positive influence on the youth. They feel they have to teach them the right way. Just being you will be an influence. And, if you are willing to listen, you will communicate that you care.

3. *Do you care about these youth? Do you really want to work with them?*

It is easy to say "Of course I care." But, when it comes right down to giving time and energy, you might find yourself wondering whether or not you really do want to work with them. What is your motivation for saying "yes" when asked to take the junior highs?

People may say "yes" because:

—they feel obligated. They may not have taught church school in the last eight years.
—they feel guilty saying "no."
—they appreciated what leaders did for their children, so they want to do their share in return.
—nobody else will do it.

And, some say "yes" because:

—they love that age group.
—they would like to know more about that age group.
—they like working with youth.
—they want to be a part of the church's ministry with youth.

If you really want to work with this age group, you will have a good time. Junior highs can sense the level of your interest.

4. *How confident are you?*

Can you acknowledge your own capabilities? Are there some things about which you can say "I know something about that," or "Yes, I have some talent in that area"? You might try listing those things—subjects, activities, attributes—on which you would rank yourself highly, and then make a list of those you would rank low. If your "low" list is much longer than your "high," you most likely are underestimating yourself. Try again. We're not looking for modesty.

At the same time, it is important to accept the fact that there are things you do not do as well as the next person. And, that's all right.

5. *Can you admit that you don't know something?*

Junior highs appreciate an adult who can say "I don't know." They have had, at some point in their school career, teachers who managed to bluff through questions they could not answer. In keeping with the notion that youth seem to be smarter each generation, you can bet that they can spot a phony. They can relate to an adult who is genuine, who is not trying to play the role—"I'm the adult; you're the child."

On the other hand, I am not suggesting you try to be a "buddy" or "one of the gang." Again, they can spot a phony, in this case, the one who is trying to be "cool" and use all the "in" language. *Youth want you to be yourself.*

6. *Can you be open and honest with the youth?*

In the preceding questions, we have been talking about being open in talking about yourself and your opinions and about being honest when you haven't the answers. It was also suggested that you not be an authority, a disciplinarian. So you ask—What do you do about discipline? Maybe this is the time to deal with that question.

Junior highs are noisy, restless, and mischievous. There are bound to be problems. How can you accomplish anything if you are not to be a disciplinarian? If you have been open, honest, and genuine with them, then you must be honest about your attitude towards their behavior. Hopefully, the approach taken in this book with regards to activities and methods will remedy much of the discipline problem. But, there will be times when you can't stand the "fooling around." At that point you must simply tell them how you feel. (There is more about this in chapters 2 and 3.) You would basically have to toss the problem back at them, saying: "Hey look, we've got to work something out," or "We're just wasting time." Together, you solve the problem.

7. *Can you be flexible and innovative?*

"Flexibility" is the key word in junior high work. Expect the unexpected. Now I know that that is an illogical statement, because the unexpected by nature cannot be expected, and if it could be expected, it would not be unexpected. In the case of junior highs, it's logical: *Expect the unexpected.* No matter how hard you work at planning, there will be times when your plans will go down the drain, and you will have to do something else.

Being innovative does not necessarily mean being creative, as in "the ability to come up with new ideas every week." Rather, it means being willing to try new ideas and new methods you might find in other materials. Are you willing to let the group experiment with new ideas?

Suggestion: Make a file of ideas. You may see something in a magazine or come across materials you could use. Keeping a file helps in the confidence department.

Are you still interested?

The most important factors in taking on this job are:

> Genuineness —being YOU
> Openness   —willingness to listen and to explore new ideas
> Commitment—based on a sincere interest in and care for these kids.

One more question: Are you willing to seek help and training? Workshops and training labs seem to be fewer and far between and take place further away from wherever you are. At the same time, those who lead workshops are complaining about the low attendance. It is very hard to schedule training events these days. Time is precious to everyone. There is no day of the week suitable for any gathering of youth leaders in any town, city, district, etc.

There are excellent events on a national level, such as Locke Bowman's Teaching Skills Institutes, and annual youth leaders' conferences sponsored by the various denominations. These are usually four–seven days in length and rather expensive (especially when you add in the plane fare). They are staffed by outstanding leaders in the field. If you are involved with youth, you should try to attend one of these specialized events. Check around, though; some would be more highly recommended than others. Your church may be willing to bear some of the expense burden.

Some of you may not be able to get away to a training event. So, you will have to seek help from any trained youth leader or D.C.E. you can find. I repeat: *You* will have to *seek* the help. A very frequent problem in the enlistment of leaders is that the church promises to support you and doesn't.

Please don't wait around for the D.C.E. or whomever to check on you. *Call them! Make* them help you. You can't afford to be timid in this respect. I am speaking as one D.C.E. who frequently got too busy to call on those wonderful people who worked with the youth. How I wish I had met with them more, shared some new ideas, or just picked up the phone. I appreciated a youth leader who would call me. For one thing, it showed that he was concerned enough about his job and the kids to get help. And, it let me know how he was doing.

YOU DON'T HAVE TO GO IT ALONE

As I read through new curriculum and hear about ideas for youth programming, I keep having the same reaction: Sounds great, but, it's too much for one person. I was recently reading about a very ambitious communicant training program. It was obvious that many hours had gone into planning and arranging quite exciting sessions. A team of leadership was involved, not just one or two persons. My problem is how to encourage you to build a youth program and not overwhelm you with work.

You are going to have to help me with the answer. You will have to find what we will call a "support group" for your involvement with the junior highs. I am not saying that you can't do it alone; maybe you can, but it would be nice to have someone "in it" with you. Let me outline some possibilities.

1. In chapter 4 on planning, I suggest that you keep a list of persons who could work with you on certain activities, such as retreats and church-ins.

2. Keep in communication with the junior high church school teachers and any others (choir director) who have contact with your group. You

might be able to coordinate activities. You both will have experiences and insights to share.

3. When you do have some ideas which will take a lot of work, ask the church school council, youth division chairman, D.C.E., etc., to help you find people to work with you. Explain your ideas so that they can and will support you.

4. Youth can help you, too. Involve them in planning. Wherever you see a task they can do, ask them to do it. Keep your eye out for high school and college students who might be available.

5. This fifth possibility concerns your personal needs for support. Some persons find that being a part of a small group which studies, prays, and shares experiences and feelings is a vital part of their relationship to the church. They receive the kind of encouragement and feedback that makes it possible for them to carry out their leadership commitment.

Some persons have found that a daily prayer and study time meets their needs. They find it impossible to drum up enthusiasm every Sunday night without this sustenance. It keeps them from being "Sunday Christians" and helps them relate their understanding of the faith to their work with the youth.

One or the other—or both—of these means of support may be helpful to you. It may be the necessary factor to make your work with youth an enjoyable experience.

Consider these possibilities. Find out how you can get the support you need. You may not know exactly what you need until you have been with the youth for several weeks. So, when you sense frustration coming on, seek support. *Don't let the church let you down.*

One more word about seeking help. Make sure they hear you. Not only have I not called youth leaders, but I have failed to hear them calling me. Comments about the youth group are often made in passing when the D.C.E. or minister has many things on his mind. Unfortunately, he doesn't hear the leader saying: "I need help!" This may happen to you. It may frustrate and anger you. But, for the sake of the youth, don't give up. DON'T LET THE CHURCH LET YOU DOWN!

> You are a child of God.
> You are loved by God.
> You are unique.
> You have gifts and talents.

God has given you the gifts of power and love. It is because of him that you have what it takes to work with youth.

2

Who They Are

Junior highs are fantastic! At least, I think so. I wonder if everyone feels the same as I do. Probably not. Would you believe it if I told you that a good number of adults are afraid of junior highs? This fact is evident from the reactions of those who are asked to work with junior highs. They see them as rowdy, restless, silly kids who are impossible to handle. Adolesence—young adolescence: that impossible age, where youth are neither children nor adults. They are moody one minute and loud and aggressive the next. They are silly and sophisticated. They are a complex age group. Thus, they seem like a difficult bunch. That is the pessimistic viewpoint.

The optimist (what I would like to call "the realist") sees them as enthusiastic, open, energetic, fun, lovable, and ready for life.

The best view is to see them as individuals; unique; bringing to the group their own ideas, feelings, and creativity. It would be a mistake to lump all junior highs together and give you a list of their characteristics.

So, how are you to know what to expect? Suppose your only experience with young people had been with fourth graders. You would need to know something about junior highs in order to work with them.

There are books available which describe characteristics in great detail. Edward Sealy, in *Teaching Early Adolescents Creatively: A Manual for Church Teachers,* devotes 51 pages to a description of the physiological, sociological, and psychological development (intellectual and emotional) of this age group. Robert Browning, in *Communicating with Junior Highs,* describes patterns of growth from year to year (ages 11–13). There is an excellent chapter on growth and development in adolescence in *Parish Planning for Grades 7–10,* edited by James E. Simpson.

Rather than approach this subject as an authority, which would be presumptuous on my part, I will pass on to you reactions of junior high leaders to the following two questions:

1. *What do you like about junior highs?*

—There is never a dull moment.
—They don't "know everything" yet.
—They're open.
—They are spontaneous.
—They are honest. They say what they think and feel.
—They are not as serious as senior highs.
—They are individuals. Even though they try to conform in many ways, they are different from each other.
—They are smarter than we think they are.
—They are exuberant.

From one who has worked with both senior highs and junior highs:

> I really prefer junior highs. They are much more enthusiastic. It's easier to try out program ideas with them. Senior highs, at least many of them, give the impression they are bored. With my senior highs, when they arrived Sunday nights, I always felt like they were sitting back, saying: "Okay, entertain me." Junior highs are so energetic. They are the complete opposite at the beginning of their meetings. It's a trick to get them to stop entertaining me and each other, and to get on with what we're going to do.
>
> People talk about kids being apathetic these days, towards the church, school, everything. I see that in senior highs, but not in the junior highs. That's what's exciting to me about these live wires. They haven't been out of childhood long enough to become apathetic and cynical.
>
> Senior highs seem to be much more conscious of looking foolish. They've got to be sophisticated. They don't participate, for fear of what their friends might think of them. Junior highs will say anything. In fact, they make it much easier for me to look foolish.

Junior highs are an exciting challenge in the church. They have the enthusiasm for working on church-related projects. They reflect very deep commitments to the Christian faith. They are anxious to know more about God, about life, and about themselves. They are ripe. They have not yet formed negative attitudes toward the church. Here is an opportunity to build positive relationships, to involve young persons in the work of the church before they get "turned off."

2. *What do you find difficult about working with junior highs?*

—Keeping their attention.
—Their different levels of maturity.
—Their awkward age (not children and not adult).
—Getting them to listen to each other and not talk all the time.
—They are under peer group pressure.

The one recurring problem reported by junior high leaders is the fact that the youth are noisy all the time. The leaders get tired from yelling (not necessarily yelling at them, but yelling in order to be heard above the roar). It is hard to get them to listen. The only solution I know is: (a) good planning and (b) openness about the problem.

(a) Good planning. Having the activities of the evening well planned is essential. Plan for as much group participation as possible. Stay away from lecture. Then, the only yelling you'll have to do is the "instructions" for the activity.

(b) Openness about the problem. Early in the season, the group should be confronted with the problem of rowdiness (in whatever form). Be open with them. Tell them it is frustrating for you and a waste of time for them. Face the fact that you only have ____ hours a week together, and it could be a real waste.

Ask them to suggest solutions to the problem. Use newsprint or blackboard to write down their suggestions. Say "We need a lot of alternatives, so what are your ideas?" If they are slow at responding, start off by writing down one or two of your own, like: "I could yell and get mad." This is obviously a bad solution, so it should prod them into finding good ones.

They should work out with you an agreement by which they will take responsibility for their participation in the activities. This may eliminate, or at least minimize, the problem.

The two best ways for you to find out what junior highs are like are: (a) talk with other junior high leaders (past leaders in your church, youth leaders in other churches, public school teachers); (b) get to know the individuals in your own group.

(a) Talk with other junior high leaders. Ask them the two questions: "What do you like about junior highs?" and "What do you find difficult about working with them?" It would be interesting to compare the reactions of school teachers who see junior highs five or six hours a day, five days a week, with church teachers and leaders who see them one or two hours a week.

If you have the opportunity, visit a junior high school where your youth attend. This is where they spend about 45% of their waking hours. There you will see their peer group, the "teen scene" in action. These kids are the peers of *your* junior highs. Such a visit is quite mind-boggling when considered in relation to values, youth culture, and the role of the church.

(b) Get to know the individuals in your own group. The Value Process mini-course, p. 103 of this book, is designed with a two-fold purpose. First, to help the youth in clarifying their own values, to discover their own ways of making decisions. Secondly, it is designed to help you get to know them, the way they think, their opinions and their values related to various issues. *Values Clarification: A Handbook of Practical Strategies for Teachers and Students,* by Sidney B. Simon, Leland W. Howe, and Howard Kirschenbaum, is an excellent resource containing 79 value exercises. Many of these exercises can help you in getting to know the junior highs.

Other valuable exercises in "getting to know each other" have been created by Lyman Coleman, author of the Serendipity books (*Groups in*

Action, Breaking Free, Celebration, Beginnings, etc.). Group building exercises are described on p. 61.

Use the time at the beginning of each meeting, when youth are arriving, to get to know them individually. Do ask about school, sports, and other interests, but don't stop there. Several young people have told me they sense phoniness when the teacher/leader always asks about last night's game. Carry on a conversation, as in TWO-way conversation. If you are having trouble on a particular night, feel free to try an open-ended statement, like: "If I were to ask you _____, what would you say?" The blank can be:

> —where you would rather live.
> —where you would go if you could go anywhere for three months.
> —what was the best movie you've seen and why.
> —when you would have rather lived: 1890, 1920, or 1950.
> —what you would do if I gave you 100 dollars.

Use these or make up your own. Then go around the group, letting each person finish the statement. These are fun to use with those who arrive early.

WRITE IT DOWN WHEN YOU GET HOME

It will help you if, when you get home after each session, you write down information about each young person and some reactions you have about junior highs. If you can remember certain things about each youth, you will have something to talk about the next time you see him. You can ask him about the fishing trip, or about his new job after school, etc.

I have a friend who is married to an executive and travels all over the country to meetings. In her hotel room, she writes down the names of the people she meets and a few notes about each—where their children are in school, that they are building a new home, etc. Then, when she travels to that city at a later date for another meeting, she studies up on the people whom she will be seeing again. Now, you can imagine how impressed you would be if someone you had met a year ago asked about your daughter at Stanford. Junior highs are much the same. They need to know adults who are interested in them. The more you learn about them individually, the better the relationship you can build.

WHAT IS THE JUNIOR HIGH'S WORLD LIKE?

Their world is school, friends, family. Their concerns are popularity, grades, freedom, responsibility, dating. And, much of their world is the same as ours—television, movies, advertising, morality, economics, politics. What affects us does affect them.

Perhaps a sociological description of the world we live in and its effect on the early teen would be appropriate. I hesitate to draw such a picture, for it would be dated as soon as this book is published.

There is one issue that youth will always face, and that is CHANGE. Opinions, ideas, styles of life, priorities within our society will change. Young adolescence is the age when a person begins to take responsibility, to develop those values which give direction to his life, to make decisions, to choose between alternatives.

What makes this task so difficult is that we live in a world of conflicting values. Youth receive one set of values from parents, a different set from their peers, another from the church, and a variety of confusing values from society. For example, as youth are prepared for adulthood,

> families are saying: "be good, be careful, be successful."
> friends are saying: "be adventuresome, be reckless, be carefree, be 'cool.' "
> church is saying: "be a servant, be self-giving, be loving."
> society is saying: "be shrewd, be materialistic, be independent."

Which of these values will be dominant, as the youth grows into adulthood? It depends on the group which has the greatest influence. Unless he develops his own value system, that is, his own criteria for making decisions, he may make important choices in his life irresponsibly.

To compound the problem, there is a trend today to "back off." Some modern parents are letting their children think and do what they want, on the assumption that they will discover what is "right." The church, to avoid pressuring people, has emphasized freedom of choice. Schools, reacting against repressive learning situations, are utilizing open classrooms and student-oriented learning techniques.

This trend toward freedom is not bad. A person should be allowed to develop his potential, to freely discover the gifts within him. But, in the transition from "oughts" and "should nots" to freedom of choice, the youth is experiencing a great deal of confusion. As much as they want to make their own decisions, youth are seeking help and guidelines. They would love some answers. And their world is retreating from offering any.

So what am I suggesting? That you give answers? No, not exactly. Rather, that you seek answers *with* them, that you join the process of sorting out all the input a youth receives, that you become a learner. Try to help them in developing their own process of decision-making. Help them to discover what is really important to them.

Two ways you can keep up on youth:

1. Keep watching for articles on youth in newspapers and magazines. Check the "Keeping Up with Youth" section of your Sunday paper.

2. Listen to their music, to the words. Not only will you gain a few insights, you might also find songs you could use in connection with your group activities.

3

Who You Are in Relation to Them

So, what are you going to do with these unique, energetic, silly, loud kids? Are you supposed to just "have fun" with them? You know you want them to like you, but what about the responsibility you feel for their relationship to the church? (Wooops! I hope I didn't scare you.) It is true that you are a factor. But, as was mentioned in chapter 1, if you are open and sincere in your relationship with your junior highs, you'll most likely be a positive factor.

John R. Evans, Director of Church Relations at Austin College, once gave me my best advice on youth work. He said that, if you would spend just one half hour with each youth, your influence on their relationship to the church would be far greater than a whole year of Sunday night programs. It struck me as excellent advice, for I can recall dozens of people who could describe one person as instrumental in their relationship to the church. If you have a genuine interest in a young person, giving him your total attention for a half hour—in fact, giving anyone your undivided attention for a half hour—would be very effective.

At this point, consider your understanding of youth work. Take a minute to jot down what you see as the purpose of the church's ministry with young people. And, where do you see yourself fitting in to that ministry? What would be your objectivities?

Did you find yourself falling into any of the following "heresies of youth work"?[1]

1. The "future-church" heresy—dealing with young people as the churchmen of tomorrow.
2. The "numbers-game" heresy—measuring success in youth work by the number of young people who can be persuaded to be "active" in one aspect or another of the total youth program.
3. The "street-cleaning" heresy—setting up programs to keep the boys and girls off the street even though secular organizations as well as other churches are also ministering to the same young people.

4. The "stop gap" heresy—involving young people in a variety of organizations which substitute busy work for solid nurture in the faith and preparation for mission in the world.

Robert Browning, in *Communicating with Junior Highs,* has pointed out how we can dedicate ourselves to youth work for the wrong reasons.

All too often our working goals for youth ministry have been worthy, but actually sub-Christian. We have been consumed with the desire to have youth "involved"—regardless of the purpose of the activity. We have been appropriately concerned about the morals of our youth. But we make secondary goals into primary ones when we make character education, healthy group activities, or even the teaching of "correct beliefs" the major objective of our Christian nurture of youth. As a result, many young people do not know clearly the difference between their Christian faith and their general belief in a moral life in a democratic society. Too often the Christian message has been communicated in such general terms that many youth have seen little about it that is distinctive or compelling.[2]

Our work with youth *is* distinctive. We are not leading another social club. We are involved in the mission of the church, in the ministry of Jesus Christ. To bypass this important point would be to water down all that we do with young people.

You might write down some of your own ideas. What do you think youth work is all about? How can it be distinctively Christian? How can junior highs be involved in the ministry of the church? Those would be good questions to ask your youth.

To be Christian does not necessarily mean studying the Bible every Sunday night. Many leaders wish their youth would talk about God more. If you feel frustrated because your junior highs do not study the Bible or talk about God, then check your priorities again. Learning about God is important and is a top priority for education in the church. Giving youth opportunities to question and to share feelings about God is also very important. But too often we feel we are failing if our youth aren't obviously excited about God. First of all, that shows judgment on our part. Just because one does not talk about God does not mean he is not excited about him. He is not less than Christian. I have been faced with this dilemma quite often. I have envied various groups of "Jesus people" who seemed to "live Jesus Christ" with their whole being. But then, in another group who would not appear to be "enthusiastic" Christians, I have seen relationships grow, love and giving occur, and have sensed a love of God that was very real to them. So, I ask: Which is the right way? or better way? The answer seems to be: I have no right to try to judge which relationship to God is more real. Nor should I try to pattern my youth group after either one.

As each junior high is an individual, so each group of junior highs is unique. One group may love getting into Bible study. Another is primarily creative—they make banners; they put on dramas; they create worship services with multi-media. Another may have lots of service opportunities. Another finds thirty types of recreation.

You are making a big mistake if you're wishing your group could be like the church down the street. Someone once suggested I get up a touring singing group out of my junior highs. That was the "in" thing at that time with many churches in the city. I had 10–12 regulars (only 28 on the roll that year) and only four could carry a tune. Some singing group!

Ideally, your group should be involved in all these areas: Bible study, creativity, service, recreation. Keep that in mind when you start planning your year's program. (See chapter 4).

In light of the objectives and purposes you are considering, you should see your role with the junior highs as involving the following:

1. Building relationships.

2. Planning and carrying out the program/activities with the junior highs.

3. Evaluating.

4. Involving the youth—motivation.

1. *Building relationships*

(a) Between you and each person (individually) in the group. Get to know them. Spend some time with each one. You have a ministry to each one of these kids. You are the church in action for them. Be yourself. Let them know who you are. Let them know you care.

(b) Within the group. Building relationships within a group is not easy. At the junior high age, kids have their own groups of friends; and they can be very rejecting to those outside their own group. Cliques may be a problem in your group. I believe in arbitrary small groupings. Use lots of activities that break up cliques—discussion groups, study groups, service teams, whatever; and *you* decide who goes where. Car caravans are very successful events for youth groups. On a caravan, the youth are on the road for three to five days and can cover as much as 3,000 miles. What makes for success is the car groupings, which are very carefully planned out for the entire trip. Everybody shifts his seat for every leg of the trip, sometimes a couple times a day. Each car has a new small group after each shift. Thus, each youth gets to know every caravaner. Cliques do not exist. And, no one driver gains embarrassing popularity. It solves the problem of who gets to go in whose car without any hassling.

Group builders are a valuable tool for building relationship within your group. The initial exercises give individuals opportunities to tell about themselves—their past, their experiences, their ideas, opinions and feelings, their dreams, their thoughts about the future. Other exercises enable persons to affirm and strengthen each other. Ultimately, group members will care for each other and minister to those outside the group. (See "Group Builders," p. 61.)

I used to think that ministering to others was too much to expect from junior highs. After all, 11–14-year-olds are so absorbed in their own concerns, in growing and developing, that the church should be ministering to them. Thus, the aim of youth work would be: helping youth to grow in their understanding of God and their relationship to him.

This *is* part of the aim. But, we are doing junior highs an injustice if we don't encourage them to participate in the mission of the church, that is, the "outwardness" part of it—the loving and serving all people. They are capable of relating to other people's needs. In fact, most junior highs are sensitive. They hurt when others are hurt. When exposed to problems people face, they respond and are anxious to find solutions. And then, they become frustrated because they are too young to help in many cases.

However, it is easier for them to care about people at a distance than to reach out to the unpopular kid in their own youth group. It is a risk of one's popularity to be seen with "a creep," and it's natural to hear a junior high say: "I can't stand (so and so)." Even though you probably won't see your kids conquer such negative feelings, you can still aim in that direction. Not by force, of course. But, by patient concern. Show them the kind of care you hope they will show others. When your group looks at Christian implications in various issues, you needn't moralize. They can discover for themselves the Christian response.

2. *Planning and carrying out the program/activities with the junior highs*

Chapter 4 describes in great detail a process for planning. Careful planning is crucial. You will dread the meetings if you have to dream up a program every week. The planning process may strike you as rather ambitious. It may be, but it will give you a guideline to get you started.

Involving youth in the planning is an important part of youth work. It will help you in building relationships. Also, the junior highs will have a feeling of ownership of their program. It is *theirs,* not something you worked up *for* them. They will share in the responsibility. "If it flops, we all flop together."

Of course, you will be expected to be there every time the group meets. If you have to miss, it will be your responsibility to bring in a substitute. Brief the substitute on the schedule, what you have been doing, where he fits in, and which youth will help him.

Do get there early. I am very casual and nonlegalistic, except when it comes to leaders arriving after some young people are already sitting around waiting. That is quite ironic, for I have a terrible problem getting places on time. So, we all have to work at it. It really does make a difference. You will have time to lay out materials, newsprint, etc. You won't appear hassled. But, most importantly, you'll have a chance to talk with individuals as they arrive. The youth will have the impression you care, that you look forward to being with them. They're no dummies. They can sense the leader who can't wait until his year is up.

3. *Evaluating*

Evaluation should take place on several levels.

(a) First, you should be doing your own evaluation. Evaluate:

1) your role as leader
2) your goals
3) the program and activities
4) youth participation
5) the relationship of the group to the total congregation and to the mission of the church.

(b) Second, evaluate with the youth. Periodically, examine a series of programs. Using questions like the following, give the youth an opportunity to express their feelings and to make suggestions for the future.

(1) What did you like best about what we did?
(2) What did you like least?
(3) What should we have done differently?
(4) Look at your objectives. In what ways did we accomplish them? In what ways didn't we?
(5) What might we do in the future to extend or continue this series of activities?

In addition to planning, evaluation will help give the junior highs ownership of their program.

(c) You probably have a D.C.E., church school council, minister, youth division chairman, or someone on whom you call with questions and for help. Arrange with this person (or persons) to assist you in evaluation. Include other leaders or teachers in the junior high department. All of you should be checking with each other periodically to evaluate your situations.

4. *Involving the youth—motivation*

Motivation is the toughest concept to understand. Psychologists are still trying to figure out why people do what they do. In education, we want to know what is the best motivation for learning. Is it for reward? Or, could it be for the joy of learning?

What motivates you to be a Christian? Why does a young person go to youth group? What motivates his participation or lack of participation?

Since I cannot offer a satisfactory answer, let's look at what we do know about motivation in general.

Motivation: is related to one's needs.
                is related to one's values/priorities.

Consider your own motivation for being a Christian. Can you relate it to your needs? Does faith in Jesus Christ meet some of your needs? Does the church play a part? Can you relate your motivation for being a Christian to your values? Think of what is most important in your life. What do you value? Make a list. Is there a correlation between this list and your being a Christian?

On the assumption that one's needs and one's values are the basis—or, at least a basis—for motivation, how can you motivate your youth?

First, you will be looking for hints as to their needs. For example: they need

> love
> attention
> a sense of belonging
> to be liked
> to be important (a sense of worth)
> to be understood.

Stopping right here with those six needs, you would have enough information to know how to relate to your group. Right?

You're going to:

> love them
> give them attention (individually)
> help them feel a part of the group
> like them (show them they are acceptable)
> show them they are important (give them responsibility)
> try to understand them.

Then, you will be listening for what is important to them, their priorities and values. The value-related mini-courses (p. 103 and p. 121) may help. Junior highs are attracted to a youth group whose program is designed on the basis of their needs and interests. In the next chapter, you are encouraged to be sensitive to the needs of your youth and to discover their interests as part of the planning process.

One other word on motivation. In order to motivate youth—or adults, for that matter—we, the church, need to minister to the WHOLE PERSON. We should not limit our concern to any one area of need: spiritual, emotional, or intellectual. All three make up a person. All three should be considered as we relate to youth.

Junior highs should be motivated to participate if:

> they see you care
> they have some responsibility for their program
> they feel comfortable, acceptable
> their program relates to their lives.

Your responsibility may appear awfully heavy at this point. But, it would be unfair if I implied that you really won't have to do very much—unfair to you and unfair to your junior highs.

COMMITMENT

Are you committed to your involvement with the youth? Commitment means responding to your calling to this part of Christ's ministry with the intention of fulfilling your responsibility. To test your level of commitment, ask yourself:

—Are the junior highs a priority?
—How much time am I willing to give?
—Will I follow through with planning and evaluation?
—Will I make an effort to know each youth? Consider visiting in their homes, or spending a half hour with each.
—Do I sense that I have an important job in the church, that I am fulfilling a call?

4

A Process for Planning

"I just don't know what I'm going to do with my junior highs tonight."

"Okay kids, what do you want to talk about this month?"

"I asked the minister, and he didn't have any ideas either."

How often these words are spoken by junior high leaders. Either no plans are made for the year or planning is begun and never carried through. A common problem is that leaders are recruited so late that they do not have time to plan. Planning can be "made easy," provided that a process is carried out step by step. The following Planning Model is designed to encourage leaders to undertake planning, no matter when they are recruited. Those who are recruited early obviously have more time. But even if the leader is a fill-in or part-timer, he can begin the planning process and carry it through with the youth.

THE MODEL

1. Data gathering—the collecting of all the information pertaining to the group.
2. Diagnosis—analyzing the data.
3. Goal setting—what are we trying to do?
4. Alternatives—the listing of possibilities in order to reach the goals.
5. Choosing from the alternatives—considering the possibilities of each.
6. Plan for action—setting up a structure of the alternatives; drawing up a calendar.
7. Resources needed—leadership, materials; responsibilities assigned.
8. Evaluation—of the plans made. Any changes needed?

There are two stages in this Model—in the first, the leader plans by himself; in the second, he plans with the youth. Involving youth in planning is important, but it is a mistake to turn the planning entirely over to the youth, on the assumption that adults must not impose their ideas on youth. Many a youth planning meeting has flopped because the leader assumed that the youth could communicate their own needs and draw up their own program structure. Even if the youth did have some ideas, they were usually unable to carry them out, due to failure to complete the planning process. Often at a group meeting there is limited time; needs are discussed, plans made, and there is no time left to make provisions for carrying out the plans (steps 6 and 7). Without a structure for taking action, many good ideas are forgotten. It often happens that after a frustrating few months, the leader calls the group back for more planning; and the result is the same.

This model is designed for the leader to do 75% of the planning before consulting the youth. The youth join the process first by reacting to the data the leader has gathered. Then they respond to his diagnosis. If they disagree with any part, they rework his diagnosis so that it becomes their own. Likewise they react to his alternatives and are encouraged to add their own. It is essential to work all the way through this model, so that in the end the group has a schedule of their activities in all the areas of their group life.

1. Data Gathering

Data gathering is the collecting of all the information and ideas you will need. You cannot make a diagnosis of your group and their problems unless you find out all you can about them. The first questions are:

(1) Who are they—individually?
     What are they like—as a group?
(2) What have they been doing (last couple of years)?
(3) What do they see as successes?
     as failures?

Spend the first three of four sessions getting to know your group. Use the group builders suggested in Section B, p. 61. An ideal course for the first few sessions would be: "Value Process" (valuing exercises), described in Section C, p. 103. This mini-course would serve two functions:

(1) for the youth, it is a fun way to look at themselves; at what they value, and how to value.
(2) for you, it will give you much information about them. The exercises provide opportunities for each youth to express himself; you will discover what they are like individually. You will have clues as to why, for example, the aggressive one dominates the group; you will find that the shy one is not disinterested, as you had thought.

A retreat based on the Value Process suggestions along with group builders would be excellent for data gathering. (See sample retreat schedule, pp. 57–59.)

Note: It is not advisable to do any planning at this retreat. It is true that a retreat setting provides the kind of time needed for planning with youth. Such a retreat would be helpful, say, in early October, after the youth have met a few times, and you have done your part of the planning. *Effective planning cannot take place at the first meeting of the youth, either at a Sunday meeting or at a retreat.*

If facilities for retreats are readily available and several leaders are willing, two early retreats could be planned—one (for group building) right before school starts, and one (for planning) about a month later.

Retreats still prove to be an excellent option for junior highs. Enthusiasm for the church youth group reaches an all time high at retreats. If this is the case, if you try a "get-to-know-each-other"-style retreat and it is successful, plan to meet for a block of time (like three hours) soon after to do the Planning Process with the youth.

A common problem with youth retreats and conferences is that there is little follow-up planned. Once the retreat is over, we go back to our routine Sunday night program. Sometimes that first Sunday night has fragments of the enthusiasm left over and is the most well-attended Sunday night of the year. But then we settle into the old pattern, and the attendance as well as the enthusiasm tapers off each week.

Take advantage of the "high" of the retreat. The kids won't mind getting together for three or four hours, possibly on the following Wednesday, Saturday morning, Sunday afternoon or Sunday night. On Wednesday or Sunday you could plan to have a supper. Use this session for the Planning Process. At the retreat they were accustomed to longer sessions and therefore will be enthusiastic about getting the beloved group together again. Also, they will probably have had some meaningful experiences at the retreat in worship and in creative study; thus, they will be open to these areas in their planning.

Motivation has its basis in experiences. If they have just had positive experiences in what usually would have been "dull subjects," they will be motivated to create more such experiences.

Note: If you wait too long after the retreat, you've got a job of cranking up enthusiasm.

During the first month while you are finding out "who they are," you will be looking for information concerning the church's educational policy, facilities and equipment, resources, and ideas from other leaders. Some of the questions for your search might be:

(1) What are the *limits* for structure? Sunday night only? Can we have special events? special worship services? church-ins? trips? outings? recreation? What kinds of supper meetings are possibilities? Can we do a musical? a play?

(2) If your church has a regular fellowship meeting or a family night supper, can the youth be responsible for one program? Ask for open dates.

If there is no regular fellowship dinner, then find out if you can have a special evening where your youth might lead the congregation in some fun activities.

(3) What facilities are available: for church-ins, worship services, recreation, special programs?

(4) What equipment is available, i.e., projectors, screens, cameras, tape recorders, record players? Find out the procedure for securing the various items.

Find out where you can borrow what your church does not have.

(5) How much money is available?

(6) Does your church approve of your youth meeting with other youth groups? Find out names of leaders from other churches.

(7) Keep on the alert for ideas—from other leaders, from this book (see Section C), and from your head.

Begin making some phone calls.

At this point, let me introduce Larry Leader. He has just agreed to "take the junior highs" at his church. It is late August; he is busy gathering information. Throughout this section, we shall be following him as he sorts through the Process. He will be giving his reactions to the various steps. If he has any questions, we shall try to answer them.

He has just made a phone call to the associate minister of a neighboring church.

Mr. Mack, this is Larry Leader of Bakers Street Church. Rev. Ron said you have been working with your junior highs. I have just started working with ours, and we're looking for possibilities for this year. I was wondering if you'd be interested in doing some worship services, retreats, or outings together.

Not only did Mack react positively to the suggestion, but he gave Larry some workable ideas and helpful resources. With this response, Larry asked further: "Could you see us working out anything for November?" They talked about possibilities of a church-in (see p. 50) in November and decided to think through meeting together for other activities.

When you are making a similar phone call, find out what dates are open. If he is interested, tell him you will call him back when you check your church calendar. He will have to check his calendar as well. Don't let it drop. Keep in touch. You will need to make further plans with this other church.

LARRY'S REACTIONS

Phoning was much easier than I had expected. But I am a procrastinator, so I need to push myself to make calls. I keep forgetting to take pen and paper to the phone. I guess I didn't expect to find out so much.

The more people you talk with and the more phone calls you make before the planning, the more ideas you will have to motivate the youth. In the job description drawn up by junior highs (p. 3), a "must" for their leader was "that he have ideas." The question of motivation is baffling. It is so important to do the background work, the calling; find out as much as you can, as quickly as you can.

Recap: as you near the youth planning day, you should have notes on:

1) what the youth are like.
2) what they've done before.
3) what you can do with them.
   what structures are available.
   what media and other equipment is available.
4) a list of people working with junior highs.
5) some ideas.

You may have noted several ideas from other leaders. At this point, it might be helpful to look through Section C, noting what sessional topics are suggested and what activities are used. Hopefully this section will give you an idea of the issues that apply to junior highs and the types of activities suited to their abilities.

As you are gathering data, ideas of your own will be emerging. Write them down.

2. *Diagnosis*

Diagnosis and Goal Setting are linked closely together. In the diagnosis stage, we are asking: What conclusions can I draw from all the information I have? What are the needs of my junior highs, individually and as a group? Goal setting is the process of projecting into the future. It deals with the overall purposes of the group. What might our group be like at the end of the year? Goals give direction to all the group's activities.

Diagnosis calls for reflective thinking. Think about the following questions and write out a diagnosis of your group.

1. From what you know now about them, what are their needs?

2. In which areas of the church's life is there a lack of involvement by the youth?

> Worship
> Study
> Involvement with the congregation
> Service

3. What about their feelings about themselves?

4. What kinds of relationships do they have with their parents? With other adults?

5. What problems do they have relating to each other?

6. What problems do they have at school?

7. Do they need to know more about their society, the world around them?

Larry Leader is making his diagnosis of his eighth and ninth grade group.

LARRY'S DIAGNOSIS

They are from different schools, so they need time and activities which lead to their becoming a cohesive group. They need to be active; they seem "ready" for anything—any project that would get them involved with the church. They don't seem to be committed to anything. I don't really know what their priorities are. There is conflict with parents; they need a way to improve relationships. Youth group has not had much to offer; not many come.

Worship

Worship is not an exciting experience to them. They don't seem to understand worship.

Study

They sure don't know much. And they don't seem to be interested either. They need creative study; it's gotta be good to interest them. They have expressed interest in knowing what they believe, but they don't want to "study" it.

Congregation

They feel they are not a part of the total church; they need *something* to help them feel a part. They need to care about others, to be a part of the total ministry of our church. We need to find ways they can relate to the other kids who do not come.

Service

They need opportunities to get out and give to people. They are willing and interested, but have never had the chance.

LARRY'S REACTIONS

Writing the diagnosis was very thought-provoking. I found that I had learned a lot about junior highs in the first three sessions doing Value Process with them. They really do have definite opinions on a lot of things. I am looking forward to their reactions to what I wrote.

3. *Goal Setting*

The stating of goals is the hardest part of any planning process. It is often the point at which planning falls apart. There are several criteria for the writing of clear, attainable goals. It takes a lot of practice to be able to transfer hopes and dreams into statements of purpose. Instead of dealing with the actual setting of goals in specific terms at this time, the following questions are designed to help you envision the direction your group might take.

1. What would you like to see happen in this group? (Be as idealistic as you like, even if you have to come down to earth later. This is a good chance to *dream*.)
2. Picture what the group will look like at the end of the year. Jot down some things they may have done in the four areas:
   Worship
   Study
   Involvement with the congregation
   Service
3. Go through your notes on diagnosis and translate the needs into statements of goals.

LARRY'S EXPECTATIONS

For the next year I picture: an enthusiastic group; they enjoy getting together; they are free to express themselves; they include the new persons in the group; they reach out to those who don't come very often; they like to call their friends and get them to come.

They are youth who have grown closer to the Church, both because they have a more meaningful personal faith, and because they really care about others in the church. They care about how the church reaches out into society to do something about injustice, to bring love to society.

Worship

They will have had four creative worship experiences—one in November, one at Christmas time or New Year's, one at the beginning of Lent, and one at Easter. Two were with other church youth, of which one was a part of a church-in. They will have led the worship service on Sunday morning. They visited a Jewish temple one Friday night; they compared the Jewish service with their own.

Study

Did a unit in connection with their church school class on the beliefs of our denomination. Had an all-day Saturday workshop on "An Overview of the Bible." Did a study on Jesus—how he related to other people.

Congregation

Presented a Christmas play on Sunday morning. Led a fun night program for the fellowship dinner. Sang a cantata with the Adult Choir for Easter; those who didn't sing made banners and worked on audio-visuals. Helped in the planning of a Seminar on Values with the adults; they also participated. Ideas came from "Values: Theirs, Mine, and Ours," Section C, p. 121.

Service

Several worked in the County Home program. Some adopted a grandparent; some wrote letters for the elderly; some ran errands. We had four Saturday mornings where our group helped at the Food Distribution Center. They packed food, scrubbed floors, and did other odd jobs. We had a Service Organization sign-up. Each committed himself to doing odd jobs for the various fund drives. Made toys for the Children's Home; planned a picnic with the children. Had a Car Caravan to Atlanta to see the work of the church in that city.

Our Group

We saw our group grow through:

The car caravan
Value Process
Identity mini-course
Skating and bowling parties
Pizza and ice cream parties
The all-night church-in
The worship services
The writing of self-contracts and commitments
Youth involvement in the planning and development of their program.

LARRY'S REACTIONS

I felt like I was really dreaming. But I can see some exciting prospects for the year. I've got one problem. I am realizing that if the group were to do half of these activities, I'd have to be a full-time youth leader. I hate to bring this up, but I thought I signed up for "Sunday night only."

NOTE TO LARRY

Unfortunately, when recruiters ask an individual to be a leader of a youth group, they try to make it sound easy by saying: "It's every Sunday night until school is out." It would be wonderful if a recruiter could tell him that the youth leader is an important part of the church's ministry and thus will receive lots of support. If he wants to do a drama, so-and-so will help; or if a retreat, call so-and-so. But, that rarely happens. Recruiters consider themselves lucky if one person says "yes" to anything. They usually cannot give you a list of support people. If that is your case, but you are still interested in seeing your junior highs have a great year, then accept the fact that you will have to find your own help. So many retreats and special activities never happen because additional leadership cannot be found. Junior highs are very active and at times too much for one person. I hate to see their enthusiasm and involvement die because "we can't find anybody to help you."

Larry, you seem to like those junior highs. I hope you will tell a lot of people of the potential in that age group. Keep an eye out for people of various talents; you will need them.

Now, how do you translate this beautiful picture of a projected year with the junior highs into stated goals? As was mentioned previously, goals are important. It is necessary to be specific about what is going to happen during the year.

Goals: (1) remind us of the directions we are taking; they keep us on top of things. (2) give us criteria for evaluation. Read over your ideal picture of the group. Using the following guidelines, try to transfer your picture into usable goals.

1. A goal should be stated in terms of *student behavior*. What will they have accomplished by the end of the year?

2. A goal needs to be stated in *measurable* terms. It should be stated in such a way that you will be able to tell whether or not it has been achieved. Use *verbs* that suggest *action*.

Examples:	to discover	rather than	to know
	develop		feel
	participate		understand
	compare		learn
	contrast		be aware of
	lead		consider
	state		grow
	create		
	evaluate		

The latter list contains verbs that would be difficult to evaluate. How can you tell whether they "understand" something or "feel" something? Goals should explain what the persons will be able to *do*.

3. A goal needs to be *relevant*. Is it based on the actual needs of the youth? Does it relate to their present situation? to the church as it is today? to the present culture and society?

4. A goal must be *attainable*. Is it possible for the goal to be achieved?

5. A goal needs to be *specific*. An example of too general a goal would be "that they be Christians."

Think about these guidelines as you write out goals for your group. Then use them to evaluate your goals after you have finished. Larry is going to give it a whirl.

LARRY'S GOALS

I am stumped. You are right; this isn't easy. It's trying to use the active verbs that's getting me.

The Group:

1. That they develop a value system by examining their own values, the values of the world, the values of their parents and by examining all these in the light of the Christian faith.

2. That they discover new ways of relating to adults.

3. That they discover new ways of relating to those in their community, outside the church.

4. That they discover new ways of becoming a cohesive group.

5. That they participate in projects which require a commitment on their part.

6. That they coordinate what they know about the Christian faith with what they know about themselves, and thus find ways of putting their faith into action.

Worship:

1. That they plan, create, and develop two or three worship services.
2. That they compare their denomination's worship practices with the Jewish practices.

Study:

1. That they be able to explain the beliefs of their church.
2. That they compare the relationships Jesus had with the various people he encountered.

Congregation:

1. That they plan and lead a fun night program for a fellowship dinner.
2. That they participate in the Easter cantata presentation.
3. That they plan and participate in a Seminar on Values.

Service:

1. That they become acquainted with the elderly in the community by participating in the projects at the County Home.
2. That each person in the group work one Saturday morning at the Food Distribution Center.
3. That they be able to describe the work of the church in the city through an audio-visual program which they produced as a result of the Car Caravan to Atlanta.

LARRY'S REACTIONS

I found some were easier to write than others. Those in the areas of Congregation and Service were very easy. The project itself served as the goal. It could be evaluated once it was over. I find myself wanting to write: "that they *know* or *learn*," i.e., "That they know about Jesus' relationship with certain people."

NOTE TO LARRY

You did an excellent job. You've got the right idea. Now try going on to Step 4, Alternatives.

4. *Alternatives*

Recap: You know quite a bit about your youth. You know from persons in Christian Education at your church what is available in the way of structure, equipment, and resources.

You know which of the options (chapter 5) are open to you.

You have many ideas (hopefully) from your head, from this book, and from other leaders.

In fact, when you were goal setting, you listed several things that would come under "Alternatives."

Alternatives are those activities and methods which could be used to accomplish our goals. Alternatives are chosen in the light of the goals. Look over your goals and work with the following guidelines:

1. Do I need to determine the structure?

If you have a Sunday night basic structure and you know what other options are open to you, your structure problem is solved. However, if your church wants to change its structure with youth, you will need to meet with the education committee to determine the structure. Possible options are suggested in chapter 5, p. 45.

2. With the structure in mind, go over all that you have listed under Goal Setting, jotting down various ideas. For each goal, list the alternatives, the possible activities through which the goal might be achieved.

3. Add more. Think. Brainstorm.

Look through the Mini-Course Section (Section C).

Check the methods chapter (chapter 6).

LARRY'S PLANS

We have a regular Sunday night structure. The junior highs meet at 6:00 P.M. for a sack supper. They have an hour for their program or activity. We might be able to make it an hour and a half, 6:30–8:00. We are free to do any special events, projects, worship services, retreats. Alternatives about the group in general:

1. Goal—That they develop a value system by examining their own values, values of the world, of parents, and by examining all these in the light of the Christian faith.

> Value Process, see p. 103.
> Values: Theirs, Mine, and Ours, p. 121.
> Identity, p. 136.
> The Future of Me, p. 153.
> In God We Trust; In Christ We Live, p. 192.

2. Goal—That they discover new ways of relating to adults.

> Values: Theirs, Mine, and Ours, p.121.
> Lead fun night for fellowship dinner.
> Adult-youth seminars—on Values, on Issues (race, poverty, education, drugs).
> Bowling night with mixed teams (adult/youth).
> Adult/youth planning of entire church educational program.
> Task forces (adult/youth on various concerns).
> Forum on Leadership Roles in the Church (elders, deacons, committee members, teachers).
> Improvisational drama with adults, p. 128.

3. Goal—That they discover new ways of relating to those in their community, outside the church.

> Study on Poverty, Race, Authority, Justice. (See *Service*.)

4. Goal—That they discover new ways of becoming a cohesive group.

Use of group builders, p. 61.
Value Process, p. 103.
Pick-up meetings or parties.
Assign-a-kid (Each junior high would be responsible for contacting one
    other person).
Church-in, p. 50.
Skating parties, bowling.
Other recreation.
Retreats.
Singing.
Writing of self-contracts and commitments.
Car caravans, p. 55.

5. Goal—That they participate in projects which require a commitment
on their part.

The writing of self-contracts and commitments, p. 78. (See *Service and
    Congregation*)

6. Goal—That they coordinate what they know about the Christian
faith with what they know about themselves, and thus find ways of putting
their faith into action.

All the alternatives suggested under the four areas should be evaluated in
    the light of this goal.

Worship

1. Goal—That they plan, create, and develop two or three worship
services.

November—as part of Church-in, with another church.
New Year's Eve—with another church.
At the beginning of Lent.
Easter—early morning, with breakfast.

2. Goal—That they compare Jewish worship service and their own.

Visit Jewish worship service.
Interview a rabbi.
Interview a minister of own denomination.
Study on worship.
Study on Judaism, see p. 204.
Plan and lead a creative worship service for total congregation on Sunday
    morning.

Study

1. Goal—That they be able to explain the beliefs of their church.

Mini-course on What Do We Believe?, p. 179.
Mini-course on Our Church, p. 173.
Saturday workshop—Overview of the Bible, p. 184.

2. Goal—That they compare the relationship Jesus had with the various people he encountered.

> Mini-course on Those Who Encountered Jesus, p. 201.
> An Easter Special—Creative drama about Jesus' confrontations (they create it).

Congregation

> Fun night program
> Easter cantata with adult choir
> Seminar on Values
> Christmas play—Sunday, church school hour
> Other adult/youth seminars
> Forum on Leadership Roles in the Church
> Youth participation in committees and task forces
> Teaching—as aides, team teaching
> New member assimilation (They are trained with the adults and are responsible for junior high members of new families)
> Caroling to our shut-ins
> Easter caroling to our shut-ins
> Ushering

Service

1. County Home project

> Singing at Christmas, Easter, anytime
> Writing letters for the residents
> Running errands
> Making of articles—carry-all bags, decorative boxes, etc.

2. Food Distribution Center, Saturday morning

> Packing boxes
> Scrubbing floors
> Doing odd jobs

3. Car Caravan

> Visit agencies
> churches with inner-city ministries
> projects

4. Service Organization Sign-up

> Folding envelopes, whatever is needed

5. Children's Home

> Make toys
> Picnics
> Recreation

For all of these commitments and self-contracts may be written.

LARRY'S REACTIONS

I had no idea there could be so many possibilities. And I could probably find more if I keep looking.

At this point you have completed 75% of the work involved in planning. You are prepared to meet with the youth. You have the kind of information and ideas which should motivate the youth to take an active part in planning their year. Your setting for planning with the youth could be a retreat. (See "Retreats," p. 52.) Or, you could have a planning meeting, which often is the more feasible of the two options. It will need to be a meeting of at least three hours (included in which is thirty minutes for supper). In fact, to complete the process, thirty or forty minutes will be needed at the following meeting. The time element will vary depending upon the size of the group. If there are less than ten people, there is the possibility of completing all eight steps at one meeting. The leader must be ready to adjust his plans to the size of the group.

The remaining part of this chapter describes the planning session with the youth. The following illustration of a Sunday night planning meeting indicates the progression of the remainder of this chapter.

5:00 P.M. Leader introduces the planning model.

Shares his *diagnosis* (using newsprint).

The youth react to their diagnosis and change it.

Leader shares his year-end picture and the *goals* he has stated. (Newsprint)

Again the youth react and change.

5:30 P.M. The group is divided into five small groups.

Each group is assigned an area:

The group
Worship
Study
Involvement with congregation
Service

Each group examines the goals in its assigned area.

They look at the leader's suggested *alternatives* and add their own.

From the new list of alternatives, they discuss the possibilities of each and *choose* those which could be carried out.

6:15 P.M. Dinner

6:45 P.M. The alternatives for each area are set before the entire group. Priorities are established, working with each area separately.

7:15 P.M. A large *calendar* is displayed. The alternatives chosen in each area are tentatively placed on the calendar.

7:45 P.M. Assignments are made. Each person becomes responsible for a particular alternative, for a part of the year's program. When the time comes for the planning of a particular event, mini-course, etc., the respective "responsible person" will be called upon.

The remaining steps in the model are:

Part of Step 7—Deciding what resources and leadership are needed.

Step 8—Evaluation.

To complete the process, it is essential that these two steps be carried out at the next meeting of the group.

Agenda for the next meeting:

1. Look at the calendar. Are there any changes which need to be made?
2. Recall "responsible persons" for each project.
3. For each alternative (project, event, mini-course), decide what resources and leadership will be needed.
4. Evaluate the entire process.
   Encourage the youth to evaluate each step.
   (See questions for evaluation on p. 40.)

Even if you happen to finish the planning at the first meeting, or if you had a planning retreat, it still would be advisable to review the "responsible persons" and display the calendar at the next meeting. This gives those who missed the planning meeting a chance to take part. It also emphasizes the importance of planning by reviewing and displaying a well-organized program for the entire year. Hopefully the junior highs will have something to say when asked: "What are you doing in your youth group?"

As soon as you have determined the time and place for your planning meeting, you will need to do a few things in preparation.

PUBLICITY

1. Start announcing the coming meeting early. Publicize it at the regular meetings two or three weeks in advance. Announce it in the church school classes the Sunday before or on the same day if it happens to be scheduled for a Sunday night.

2. Send a post card to all junior highs informing them of the meeting. Include:

who—the group it concerns
what—name of meeting, purpose
when—both the time you expect to start and the time you expect to end
where—place and address

Here is a sample, but I am sure you can think of something more creative.

ATTENTION: ALL 7th, 8th & 9th graders

BIG PLANNING MEETING

Sun., Oct. 3, 19—   at David & Beth Barnes

5:00–8:00 p.m.   26 Rockford Lane

Plans for the entire year will be made.

See You There!

Send the card out about four or five days before the meeting. This card serves as a reminder and should not be sent out too early.

3. Get a few to phone others on the day of the meeting or at least on the day before.

GETTING YOURSELF READY

1. Picture the meeting. Go over the schedule. What will you do first? Try to imagine the unexpected. What will you do if only four people show? Picture what it would be like if thirty or thirty-five came.

Note: If four or less is your attendance, I would suggest you bag the planning—you must have picked the wrong night—and find an ice cream or pizza place. At least you'll get to know four of your junior highs better.

2. Your biggest job will be preparing the newsprint sheets. The best way to share your information with the group is visually. Secure a large flip chart for this purpose. Newsprint, i.e. flip charts, may be found at school supply stores, hobby shops, or possibly at your church. On the flip chart sheets you will need to:

   a. Reproduce the PLANNING MODEL (all eight steps).
   b. Write out your DIAGNOSIS.
   c. Write out your YEAR END PICTURE.
   d. On the next few sheets, state a GOAL at the top of the page and list beneath it the ALTERNATIVES you have found.
   e. Make a large CALENDAR of the months ahead. You could use three sheets with three months on each. Make sure the calendar is big enough for the group to see the days and weeks of the month. You could use poster board instead of newsprint.

3. Regarding the supper, whatever kind of supper you are planning, line up someone else to handle the preparation of the meal, so that you are completely free to spend your time with the group.

THE MEETING

Materials needed: flip chart, poster board (optional), felt pens, easel or masking tape.

5:00 p.m. It would be unrealistic to expect everyone to arrive on time. Since you will need all the time allotted, try to begin as soon as possible. The first activity is your explanation of the Planning Process Model. After you have explained it, display it (on easel or by taping it to a wall), so that late comers may refer to it.

After explaining the model, go right into sharing your DIAGNOSIS with them. If the junior highs were restless or inattentive at first, their curiosity will settle them as they become eager to find out "what you think about them." Encourage them to agree or disagree. They should be very responsive, especially when you hit upon something they disagree with. This part of the process will set the atmosphere for honest participation by the youth.

Note: Tell them your diagnosis item by item, *without* using the newsprint. If they see your diagnosis written out, they may jump ahead of you. After you have stated the diagnosis, then display it on the newsprint and make the changes they suggest.

Do the same procedure with the YEAR END PICTURE. Explain to them that you have really been dreaming and are about to read a description of the fantastic year they will have had by June next year. Again, save the newsprint until after you have finished telling them the year end picture. Ask if they have any changes to make in the dream. Would they like to add something? Give them some time to think.

Ask if any of them have ever done any GOAL SETTING. Perhaps a few have and would explain how they went about it. In order to share your goals, you could (1) read them slowly one by one without using newsprint; (2) cover the list of alternatives on your goal-alternatives sheets with poster board, so that you can show the goal without revealing the alternatives; or (3) display a list of all the goals on a separate sheet of newsprint.

Point out the importance of having goals to give direction to the various activities. Ask them to react to, change, and add to your goals.

Note: Thinking in terms of goals may be a relatively new experience for the junior highs. They may have very little to say in reaction to your goals. Don't spend too much time trying to engage them in goal setting. As they take part in the activities throughout the year, they should be referring to their goals. Also they will need to look at the goals when they evaluate the various aspects of their program. By the end of the year they should have a much clearer understanding of this process and should be capable of setting some of their own goals for the following year.

5:30 p.m. If there are more than ten junior highs present, you can divide them into five smaller groups. Obviously they might be very small groups (perhaps duos or trios). Ahead of time you will need to have divided your goal-alternatives sheets somewhat equally. The areas are: (1) worship; (2) study; (3) involvement with the congregation; (4) service; and (5) the group. The last category will include all the goals

that pertain to the group as a whole, such as growth of the group, recreation, relationships to adults, parents, peers. You may want to use only
four small groups. You would then distribute the "group" goals among the
four groups. No matter how you divide the goals, make sure that all the
groups have fairly equal tasks.

Give out the respective newsprint sheets of GOALS-ALTERNATIVES.
Give the groups the following instructions:

> Examine the goal.
> You are to find alternatives that would accomplish the goal. Listed on the
> sheet are several possibilities. Think of more and add them to the list.
> Discuss each alternative. Could you see us doing it this year?
> Choose those which are the best.

6:15 p.m. As the groups finish their work, they may move on into the
kitchen or wherever and get their meal. While they are eating, pick up all
their goal-alternative sheets. If possible, tape all the sheets on the same
wall, so that the group can have a comprehensive view of their work. If
not, deal with one sheet at a time.

6:45 p.m. Ask a representative from each group to share the alternatives
they have chosen. Find out from the total group what their priorities are.
Voting may be used to determine the popularity of each. Guide the group
to work quickly, so that priorities may be established in each area. They
have a half hour to work through this step.

7:15 p.m. Looking at all the alternatives which are highly ranked, start
putting them on the CALENDAR. Some will obviously be more appropriate for certain times, such as those relating to Advent, Christmas,
Easter. Put those on the calendar first. Where mini-courses (usually requir-
ing four sessions) have been chosen, arrange them over the course of the
year. Some decisions will be tentative, as you will have to find out if they
can take place at a certain time. For example, the junior highs may decide
they want to lead a Sunday morning worship service on a Sunday in
November. You will need to check with the minister and/or worship committee before confirming a date. Mark a red "X" next to those which will
need such inquiry.

With the entire calendar before the group, you should be able to create
a balanced program for the year. Recreation and parties can be well
spaced.

7:45 p.m. Time is running out. If you do not finish the calendar by
fifteen minutes before quitting time, stop and do this step (Step 7). This
step asks for commitment from the youth to their program and must be
done at this meeting.

Explain that you are going to ask for volunteers for each program, for
each alternative chosen. This volunteer becomes a RESPONSIBLE PER-

SON for this program. He will be called upon later when it is time to do the detailed planning for the mini-course, service, event, etc.

Go through each alternative that has been placed on the calendar and jot down the names of "responsible persons" for each. Make sure you have and keep this list.

At the end of this meeting you and the junior highs should have a good idea of your program for the year. But, you still have not finished the planning process. You have left it in the middle of Step 7. Plan to take approximately thirty or forty minutes at the next meeting to complete the process. Between the meetings check with the appropriate persons (ministers, D.C.E.s, people from other churches) to see if you can work out dates for those projects marked "X" for tentative.

AT THE NEXT MEETING

Display the newsprint sheet on THE PLANNING MODEL. As the junior highs are gathering, display the CALENDAR and explain to those who may not have been at the planning meeting what went on. Make sure they know you are glad they are here this week and that they can "get in on" being "responsible persons" for the several projects. They may also be interested in looking over the DIAGNOSIS, the YEAR END PICTURE, and the GOAL-ALTERNATIVES sheets.

1. With the group assembled, look at the calendar. Report what you found out about the tentative items (marked "X"). Ask: Are you satisfied with the calendar? What changes might we need to make?

2. Review the "responsible persons" for each project. At this time ask those who were not present the week before to choose some projects for which they will be responsible. You will have to explain again what the responsible person does.

Note: This may not be the right time, but at some point I would suggest that you discuss with the group the problem of continuity. A frustrating part of working with a group over a period of time is that from week to week the makeup of the group changes. As a result you must repeatedly explain what has been happening in the previous meetings. Having everyone show up every week would be ideal. But that will not happen. By pushing the planning process, by trying to involve as many as possible at the beginning of the year, there is a better chance that the junior highs will start making their youth group a priority.

If you feel comfortable with the group, bring this up. If, however, there are persons at this meeting who might be embarrassed by the subject, save it. Do talk about it soon, however, so that the junior highs will assume some responsibility for involving those who come less frequently.

Make sure you have all the newly assigned names on the calendar.

3. On a clean sheet of newsprint, write RESOURCES at the top. For

each project, event, mini-course, etc., have the group think of outside leadership, equipment, and other materials which will be needed. This does not have to be a detailed list. Try to think of items or persons which would need to be lined up early.

4. EVALUATE the entire process. Bring out the newsprint listing the eight steps of the Planning Model. Ask the following questions:

    a. How did you feel about the leader doing so much of the planning?
       Review for them what you did for:
          Step 1—Data gathering
          Step 2—Diagnosis
          Step 3—Goal setting
          Step 4—Listing of alternatives
    b. Do you feel I found out the right kind of information?
    c. What were your reactions to my diagnosis?
    d. What did you think about the idealistic year end picture?
       Is it bad to be idealistic?
       Was it that unrealistic a picture?
    e. How did you feel about goal setting?
       Can you think of other ways we could go about setting goals?
    f. What about the alternatives?
       Was it hard to think of more?
       Were your ideas taken seriously?
       How might we have handled the choosing of alternatives differently?
    g. Are you willing to take the responsibility for further planning? —Because I will be calling on you.
    h. Can you think of ways to improve the process?

If this were not a book, I would say: "Any questions?" But, since it is, and I cannot guess what your questions might be, I have included some observations from Larry Leader. He tried the 5:00–8:00 P.M. meeting on a Sunday night with his eighth and ninth graders. Thirteen showed.

LARRY'S REACTIONS

If I haven't mentioned it before, thirteen is a good attendance for our church. We have twenty-five on the eighth and ninth grade roll. Last year the average attendance was eight. Anyway, their responses to my diagnosis were hysterical. They freely agreed and disagreed, strongly disagreed (booed!). They laughed at my idealistic picture, but they never missed a word of it. They showed a lot of enthusiasm.

When we broke up into groups, I hit one problem. They did not understand all of my alternatives. So I had to go around to each group and explain several. It worked out all right; there was enough time for me to do that. But then I had to explain the same ones to the entire group when we displayed all the sheets after supper.

An interesting thing that happened was that they liked my alternatives. In fact, in a couple of groups they said they couldn't think of any to add. There were very few original ideas.

When the group got together after supper, they were very enthusiastic and did a fine job setting up their calendar. They volunteered willingly for the "responsible person" jobs. A few events did not make it to the calendar, as time was running out. However, we did assign "responsible persons" for everything that made it to the calendar.

The next week: There were fourteen people at this meeting; only six of those had been present for the planning meeting. Eight were new, as far as the planning was concerned. I was discouraged. Since there were so many who had missed the previous meeting, I did talk with them about continuity. Some had heard about the planning meeting and were anxious to find out about the "great year." They were so responsive that I decided to bag what I had planned for the last half of the meeting and spend the entire hour going through the process. I read my diagnosis, year end picture, and goals. We worked with the calendar and finished placing the remaining events. All eight signed up to be "responsible persons." We went through the resources step and evaluation. The original six offered some helpful comments. They were very enthusiastic about the process. They affirmed the need for the leader doing a great deal of the work beforehand.

NOTE TO LARRY

In regard to their not understanding your alternatives, you handled it perfectly. It may have seemed a little chaotic, but by your repetition I am sure they better understood what was going on.

It is quite common for junior highs not to have a whole lot of new ideas. They should like most of your ideas. After all, you did a lot of research. To encourage creative thinking on alternatives, one might list only two or three alternatives for each goal. If the leader has more, he could hold back a few which he could bring up later, when the group reconvenes after supper.

It sounds like you handled the second meeting beautifully. As a result, you now have twenty-one junior highs committed to their own program for the year.

This completes the Planning Process. To insure the success of your planning, a couple of follow-up items need to be mentioned.

1. You will need to send a letter to all junior highs reporting the results of their planning efforts. List the activities month by month. For each, note the names of the "responsible persons." You could personalize each letter by underlining the respective person's name wherever it appears as a "responsible person."

2. Check the calendar. Plan to telephone those who are "responsible persons" for the first month's activities. Arrange to meet with them to

plan the first mini-course, service, project, whatever. As leader your part in the planning will be similar to your part in the planning process. You will usually be doing about 75% of the work.

Note: Try to keep ahead of the activities, so that you won't get caught without the necessary resources or preparation. Recruit the extra leadership as early as possible.

Be on the lookout for various responsibilities that can be turned over to the junior highs themselves. Throughout the year you will be getting to know them better and can give them increasing amounts of responsibility.

Use of this systematic process for planning should enable you to be a more effective and less frustrated junior high leader. Not having to worry about "getting up a program" every week should free you to enjoy your group.

Section B

Options and Methods

5

Options for Structure and Special Events

This book has been written primarily in response to a call for help from leaders of Sunday night youth groups. Sunday night has been and still is the most common structure for youth ministry. It is not the most innovative, but it *is* the most common. So, as long as we have it, we need to make good use of it.

Now you may have more freedom in your church. You may be able to do something "different." In this section, we'll look at several different structures. I am sure there are more options than these, that some creative people somewhere have much better ideas. In case you don't live near any of these creative people, maybe these suggestions will help you in planning for youth ministry.

Also in this section is a description of three special events: RETREATS, CHURCH-INS, and CAR CARAVANS. These are excellent methods with junior highs. In terms of success, these three rate at the top of the list, above everything else you could do with kids.

1. Sunday Night

First, a few words about good old Sunday night. There are several possibilities for time structure:

(a) 6:00–7:30 The group can bring sack suppers or eat a prepared meal at the church.
(b) 5:00–7:30 This time is popular with groups who have study and re-creation. It gives you more time. Includes meal.
(c) 7:00–8:30
   or   Group meeting with snack served.
   7:30–9:00

Meals can be prepared by parents of youth on a rotation basis. Or, you may have a large group and a cook available. Meetings can be held at the church or in homes, usually on a rotation basis.

ADVANTAGES OF MEETING AT THE CHURCH

1. You are making use of your facilities. Church buildings are used so infrequently.
2. It affirms a visible connection with the church. Hopefully, it helps promote positive relationships between church and youth.
3. There is no misunderstanding about the place of meeting. Same time; same place.

If you do meet at the church, you should have a medium-sized room. Church school classrooms are too small. The fellowship hall is usually too large, unless you have partitions.

It's nice to have a rug. It seems easier to be a community when you're sitting on a soft floor together. I like rugs!

ADVANTAGES OF MEETING IN HOMES

1. It's homey. It's comfortable. It does facilitate community. (More rugs!)
2. The youth get to know each other's parents. They meet more of their church members. And, it gives the parents an opportunity to contribute.

If you do meet in homes, make sure everyone has the directions straight. Homes are appropriate for almost any program or activity.

Note: If you're in the process of deciding the length of the meeting, consider that one hour for program/activity is MINIMUM. One hour and a half is nice. Two hours is good, but your activities need to be well planned.

The mini-courses in Section C can be used for all three lengths. You can spend more time on certain exercises if you have two hours. If you have only an hour, you will need to eliminate some and shorten others.

By now you've probably figured that the key is *flexibility*. Some exercises won't last as long as you expected. With others, an hour will go by long before you finish. Don't let "time" get you down. If you don't finish something, don't worry about it. Be constantly evaluating. After a meeting is over and you had to omit an exercise, weigh its importance and consider shifting your plans for the next week.

Continuity is important when you are meeting every Sunday night. Both you and your group will appreciate knowing what's going to happen every Sunday night. Planning the full year's calendar is an anxiety-saver. (See chapter 4 on planning.)

There are a couple of options for Sunday night programs.

(a) The mini-course approach

A mini-course is usually four sessions. You can plan a mini-course for each month. You will have an extra Sunday every once-in-a-while. That is a good time for something extra—recreation, a trip to the pizza place or putt-putt, or a free F.O.I. (Feelings, Opinions, and Ideas), a night when they can discuss anything they like; a yak session.

It is wise to space mini-courses with a fun night between each.

(b) The Sunday-a-month approach

In this approach, you follow a schedule like the following:

    first Sunday   — a topic
    second Sunday   — a project
    third Sunday   — a film
    fourth Sunday   — recreation

I am not quite sold in this approach, although I am open. If you are having a terrible time becoming a group, that is, if you have one group the first Sunday, and a completely different one the next, this approach may solve your problem. It is hard to carry through a mini-course if you don't have enough of the same folks coming every week.

You may have extreme divergence of interests in your group. Some want to study the Bible and won't come unless you do. Some, on the other hand, would never come to a Bible study, but would for recreation. Others are interested in current issues. If this is the case, and you see no hope of getting everyone together, a Sunday-a-month schedule may be a solution.

What about straight recreation every Sunday night? There are some who claim that the kids get enough serious stuff in church school. They feel Sunday night should be recreation and unstructured fellowship. I don't want to come down too hard against this, although there was a time when I would have. I have heard plenty of kids complain that their youth group was "nothin'." "All we ever do is play volleyball." In fact, they have blamed their leaders for never planning anything. I know that's a little unfair to a lot of leaders. After all, their job isn't easy—especially if they're not getting any help or ideas.

I would suggest that you carefully evaluate your total ministry with youth. If your church is involving them on the study level, the worship level, and the service level, then the youth need recreation and times when they just have fun getting together.

Evaluation is important. You might even find that Sunday night is totally irrelevant.

2. *Interest Grouping*

Interest grouping could come under "Sunday night" or could be considered for any night or weekday. For this reason I place it in a category by itself. Interest grouping is for large churches. It is for churches with a lot of youth with a lot of interests—and a LOT OF LEADERS!

Well, maybe you are lucky and can find leaders who would like to use their talents with youth in special areas, like:

> music
> drama
> photography
> arts and crafts
> puppetry
> issues
> values clarification
> transactional analysis (if you have a qualified leader around)
> creative worship (you could have a creative service once a month, with youth leading)
> parent-youth activity/study

You could offer a six to eight weeks course in, for example, four of these. After that period, you could change—either change the courses, or, keep the courses and change the groupings, allowing persons to switch. In this way you would have four different groups meeting on any Sunday night.

The youth should sign up for these ahead and should stick with their interest group for the duration.

3. Weekday Program (Youth Club)

The weekday program usually is multi-purpose. It may have three or more parts: study, choir, recreation, crafts, supper, fellowship, worship. A schedule might be:

> 4:15 p.m.—Choir
> 5:15   —Study
> 6:15   —Supper
> 6:45   —Recreation and crafts

Not all youth are singers, so some would not come until 5:15. The study hour is often combined with communicant training.

You can use a variety of methods and activities with this structure. The youth "club" idea suggests commitment on the part of the youth. They are expected to participate every week. Lots of adults can contribute their skills in cooking, crafts, teaching, and recreational leadership.

4. Saturday (9:30 a.m.–3:00 p.m.)

A series of monthly Saturday meetings (could be called mini-retreats) are an option for junior highs. This replaces the Sunday night program. Except for special events, this is the only meeting of the youth group.

The mini-courses (Section C) can easily be adapted to this structure. The four sessions would take place in one day. The greatest advantage is in group building. Junior highs can come to church every Sunday night for an hour and a half and never feel closer to the others in the group. Five and a half hours provides an excellent opportunity for becoming a group.

Lunch is included. You can take breaks for games and recreation. If you are open for options, gather your planning group of youth and plan out a few Saturdays. This may be the structure to meet your needs.

5. *Youth Weeks*

Instead of meeting on Sunday nights, your youth could participate in three or four youth weeks. Youth week might be four or five nights— Sunday through Thursday or Monday through Thursday. The time might be 7:00–8:30.

Youth weeks are built around certain topics. A mini-course could be used for one week. A film festival for another. An art festival. You could plan a recreation week—softball Sunday night, Putt-Putt Monday, volleyball Tuesday, games on Wednesday, and bowling Thursday. You could meet in four or five different homes. There are endless possibilities.

The advantage is concentration. You are seeing the same group (hopefully) every night. The youth weeks would take planning. Make sure to get a planning group to work with you on each.

6. *Seasonal Programming*

This kind of programming takes careful planning. There is no regular time for meeting. A planning group is responsible for each season. Advent-Christmas and Lent-Easter are the two basic seasons.

The planning group first considers the four areas: worship, study, fellowship, and service. The group will need to develop activities in each of these areas and plan them for the Advent season and the Easter season. Times and places are flexible. It is totally up to you and your planning group. For example, one group did the following:

Worship—They planned a creative worship for the second Friday night before Christmas and one for New Year's Eve. Both services were held at 11:00 P.M. The entire congregation was invited.

Study—They met on the four Sunday nights in Advent and did a mini-course on "Who is Jesus Christ?"

Fellowship—They had a Christmas party in one of their homes. They went caroling. They had a church-in at the beginning of Advent. They all took part in a program and worship service for the whole church.

Service—They planned a party for a children's home. They made packets (toothbrushes, soap, etc.) for prisoners in the county jail.

The advantage of this option is its flexibility and its purpose-oriented structure. The group never met just because it was time for youth group. They had a purpose for every part of their program.

7. Retreats

Four or five retreats could be planned for the year. Again, they would replace the Sunday night structure. This option is much the same as the Saturday programming and the youth weeks. A mini-course could be the basis for the retreat. Fellowship, recreation, and worship can be included.

Advantages: continuity—same group for a longer period of time, good for group building, purpose-oriented.

SPECIAL EVENTS

1. Church-ins

There are a variety of names going around for this event—church-ins, lock-ins, sleep-ins. It is an event which takes place *at the church,* usually over a Friday night. Of course, you could have it on a weeknight during the summer.

It starts around 8.00 P.M. Friday and dies around 7:30–8:30 A.M. I say "dies," because that is what it feels like. You may have guessed it— there is really no sleep involved, or very little. I don't know how many times the youth cart along those comfy sleeping bags and never get to use them. (*Sleep*-in is the wrong word.)

It is a very structured event. The ground rule is that everyone is to participate in every activity. No one is to leave the group. *Lock*-in is the right word. They are locked in the youth building and locked-in to their group. Activities are planned continuously until 3:00 or 4:00 in the morning. If someone absolutely "flakes out" at 2:30, that's all right. But usually junior highs can stay up all night and love to have the chance.

It's ironic—on retreats you always have junior highs begging you to let them stay up. In church-ins you go until they beg you to let them go to sleep.

Now, before you start thinking this is cruel and unusual punishment, let me describe a sample church-in schedule.

The theme for this particular church-in was: THE CHURCH: A FOR REAL COMMUNITY.

8:00 P.M. Introduction Interviews (see p. 63)
8:30   Name charade—on backs (see p. 97)
8:50   Make collage describing self (p. 64)
9:30   Break—played volleyball in lighted parking lot. Refreshments
10:00   Small groups (4 groups)
               (a) Describe self by explaining collage
               (b) Respond to the following questions:
                       —What is the church? (Come up with a group definition.)

    —What activities and service projects does our church do?

    —What does Paul say about the church in 1 Corinthians 12:12–26? Paraphrase the passage without using any of the same words.

    —Using Paul's image, what part of the church are you—eye, ear, foot, hand? "I see myself as . . ." Why?

11:00 Come together

    Each group reports; Brainstorm what junior highs can do in the church

11:30 Games

    Zip Zap (see p. 97)

    A What? (p. 96)

    Operant Conditioning (p. 97)

12:00 Break; Explain that after break, small groups will work out worship

    Group 1—Call to worship—multi-media

    Group 2—Confession and prayers

    Group 3—Music

    Group 4—Scripture and communion

    Refreshments

12:15 Small groups work on worship service

 1:15 A.M. Worship preparation—group singing

 1:30 Worship service celebration

 2:15 Break

 2:30 Make movies

    Work on skits in small groups

    Film them

    Some wanted to do more, so we did more

About 3:30, a few fell asleep

    some sang with guitars

    some talked

Around 5:00, those who were still awake played a game they made up with a volleyball

At 7:30 one of the leaders went out and bought donuts, orange juice, and milk

By 8:30, everyone had eaten and packed up

 There are many more activities and methods that can be used at church-ins:

  Rent a thirty, sixty, or ninety minute movie.

  Use the clay or wire sculpture described on p. 75.

  Use group builders (p. 61) and values clarification (p. 70)

Do make movies. Let them work out skits.

Think of some lively ways to celebrate in worship—snake dance while singing.

Guidelines for Church-ins

1. Take away each person's watch. Put it in an envelope with his name on it, and put it in a safe place. Only you and one other leader should have watches. They will try to guess the time. They will beg you to tell them. It's part of the game.

2. Make sure they understand that they will be locked in and must participate in the activities. There is a little leeway—for example, not everyone has to play volleyball. But those who don't should watch and cheer everyone on. You are trying to prevent little groups from going off into a corner. Once they are off, it is hard to get them involved again.

3. Use arbitrary small groupings. When you have your list of participants, make up the list of small groups before the church-in. Do this very carefully. Break up cliques. Put shy kids with aggressive ones. Place the new kid or the one who doesn't come very often with a group where he will be comfortable. If you do not know who will be there, make up the groupings while they are busy with an activity, like making collages.

4. Be flexible. If something is not working, alter the activity. But don't be too quick to throw out your plans. The exact hours on your schedule are approximate. After all, you have all night. The time schedule gives you a guideline for the activities.

5. Have plenty of food, snacks. You will need it for survival.

Leadership can be a problem. Bet you can guess why. You may be saying to yourself, "I could never stay up all night with a bunch of junior highs." Maybe you can, and maybe you can't. See if you can find other leaders—a young couple. A college student is great.

Note: Write a letter to the parents of your group, telling them what a church-in is. Explain that the youth will be staying up all night. Adult reaction to your ideas is much more positive when you take extra steps to communicate with them.

A church-in could be the highlight of the year for your junior highs. See if you can work it out.

2. Retreats

Retreats were mentioned earlier. Retreats are very popular with junior highs and are suggested in addition to their regular programs.

Retreats are usually two or three days in length: Friday–Saturday; Saturday–Sunday; or, Friday–Sunday. By definition, in order to have a retreat, you have to "retreat" or go off somewhere, away from the hustle and bustle. The setting would be a camp or conference ground, or a large cabin. It could be held at a college.

There are a variety of ways to design a retreat. Many people feel retreats should be unstructured. The youth should have lots of free time. There is a problem with lots of free time—no, I am not thinking of mischief but, rather, cliques. If you have ever watched a group of junior highs arriving for a retreat, you will see them milling around, unpacking, checking things out, in twos or threes. And, there is usually one group of five or six who are "buddies." Let's say you gave them four hours of free time in the afternoon—free time including recreation. At supper time, the same twos and threes and the larger group of buddies would still be together. In fact, they may not have spoken one word to any of the other kids.

Now, if you had spent the afternoon doing group building exercises and small group activities, by supper there's a chance you would see evidences of group cohesiveness. Often, youth come back from retreats saying, "We didn't really do anything." This is another disadvantage of low-structured retreats. On one retreat, a junior high reported: "Both afternoons were free time and recreation. The program after supper lasted from 7:00–9:00. And, in the morning, we had a Bible study and discussion. We had an 11:00 P.M. lights out, but no one went to bed before 3:00."

The guidelines for retreats are very similar to those for church-ins. The structured emphasis seems to work better. By structure, I am not implying an inflexible, military-like schedule. But, I am suggesting making good use of the time with a wide variety of activities.

The following is an example of a junior high retreat schedule for a Saturday–Sunday:

9:30 A.M.	Leave church
10:30	Unpack
11:00	Group Builders (see p. 61)
	Name tag symbols
	Introduction interviews
	Open-ended statements in small groups
12:30	Lunch
12:45	Games—John, John, John (p. 65)
	Zip Zap (p. 97)
	Guess Who? (p. 67)
1:30 P.M.	Outdoor games and recreation
4:00	Bible study in small groups
5:00	Come together; Share insights and tasks
5:45	Break
6:00	Dinner
7:00	John, John, John again and singing
7:15	Virginia Reel conversation (p. 67)
7:45	Small groups

	Group building
	Creative activity
	Bible study
8:45	Come together; Share group work
9:15	Break; Refreshments
9:30	Group singing; Plan worship for tomorrow;
	Divide into groups; Work on audio-visuals
10:30	Make banners
11:30	Small group affirmation
	Fire (p. 67)
	Color Me (p. 68)
	Strength bombardment (p. 68)
	Design skits for presentation
1:00 A.M.	Skits
1:30 or so	Break
1:45	Games
	A movie (16 mm)
	Make movies

Bedtime around 2:30

Sunday

9:30 A.M.	Breakfast
10:00	Small groups—each group writes a prayer for worship
10:30 A.M.	Worship
11:30	Small groups
	Write letters to the group (to be mailed later) or some final group activity
12:15	Lunch
	Clean up and leave

For a one night retreat the best hours are the evening and the wee hours. Youth can function the next morning, but not usually that afternoon.

For a two night retreat, activities should go until 1:00 A.M. Group spirit is high after 11:00 P.M.; that's why I suggest making good use of that time. There is no need to get up early in the morning.

ADAPTING THE MINI-COURSES (SECTION C)

All the mini-courses have four sessions and are adaptable to retreat settings. In a two day retreat, the sessions could be held:

         4:00–5:30 P.M.   Session I
         7:00–8:30 P.M.   Session II
        10:30–12:00 A.M.   Session III
    and 10:00–11:30 the next morning for Session IV

For a three day retreat:

Session I—any 1½ hour segment on Friday evening
Session II—10:00–11:30 on Saturday morning
Session III—7:00–9:30 on Saturday night
Session IV—10:00–11:30 on Sunday morning (or late Saturday night)

DEALING WITH PROBLEMS

You should have some ground rules. The basic is: EVERYONE SHOULD PARTICIPATE IN EVERYTHING. They shouldn't be wandering off.

The "no alcohol, drugs, sex" rule, which seems to be engraved over the entrance to every retreat, can be a problem in varying degrees, depending on the group. Two suggestions:

(a) Talk about these three problems openly with the group. Ask them if such abstinence is agreeable for the retreat. You won't get serious disagreement. Ask them for suggestions on how to deal with people who may break the agreement. Emphasize that it is *their* retreat. What goes on is their responsibility.

(b) Talk with them about rumors and stories that some people enjoy telling about retreats. The point is: not whether or not these stories are true, but that these stories become the only thing people have to say about the retreat. You might explain it to the group something like this:

> You know, we might all have a fantastic time on this retreat. You've been begging for one, and it's finally here. You'll probably get to know each other really well. Some very significant things might happen in your life and in your feelings about the church. The creative worship (late tonight) might be the most fantastic experience ever.
> I would hate to think that all anybody would ever have to say about our great retreat is: "I heard some kids had some pills." We get home, and we think back on all this retreat meant to us. And, it means a lot to me too. But, you don't hear about the good things that happened. All you'll hear are some rumors.

Make this heart-to-heart speech in the evening, rather late, after you have been together for a while. It will cause them to take notice of the fact that they *are* finally on a retreat and they are having a good time. Don't talk about it right at first. It's not as appropriate. By the way, in case you haven't figured it out . . . maybe those few mischief-makers will realize that what they might have been planning to "get away with" isn't really worth it.

3. Car caravans

This has got to be one of the most enjoyable experiences for you and the junior highs. A car caravan is a trip, short or long, taken in two, three, or four cars.

WHAT'S INVOLVED?
—fun
—a learning experience
—small groups

(a) FUN—You visit a fun place on the trip, something like Six Flags Over Georgia, the Baseball Hall of Fame, etc.

(b) A LEARNING EXPERIENCE—The group usually visits projects which churches are doing in communities.

(c) SMALL GROUPS—The cars are the small groups. Each small group has an adult leader (the driver). Group building exercises are used on the road. The small group on a caravan changes every day or at intervals during a long segment of the journey. The leaders have prepared a chart for who is to be in whose car at what time.

WHERE DO YOU GO?

If you live within two or three hours of a city which has agencies connected with the church working in various areas, you might consider a two-night caravan.

If you can take four or five days or more (during Easter or summer vacation), you can make a route through three or four cities or towns.

STEPS IN ORGANIZING A CAR CARAVAN

1. Look at a map and consider the possibilities. Example: We took a car caravan of Little Rock, Arkansas, youth on a five-night trip from Little Rock

> to Atlanta
> to Montreat, N. C.
> to Nashville, Tenn.
> and back to Little Rock

Look for possible triangle routes.
Another example: from Charlotte, N. C.

> to Richmond, Va.
> to Washington, D.C.
> to Charlottesville, Va.
> and back to Charlotte

2. Talk with a couple of ministers, Directors of Christian Education, or other persons who might know of active churches in various places.

For the Little Rock caravan, we knew there was a lot going on in Atlanta:

> —the denomination's boards and agencies
> —an extensive ministry at a downtown church
> —While there, we found out about a ministry with the counter culture on the "Strip."

At Montreat, the General Assembly of the Presbyterian Church, U. S., was in session.

In Nashville, the P.C.U.S. Board of World Missions.

3. Pick a few alternant routes. Estimate travel time. Choose the dates to consider. Estimate where you might stay overnight.

4. Write letters to churches of your denomination in the cities selected. Make phone calls, if necessary. Explain that you are putting together a caravan and would like to know if any of the churches in the area are doing projects in the community, which your group might visit. Ask them what is available for lodging (how about their church floor?).

You need to do this several months ahead. If there isn't anything worth seeing in a place, you will need to reroute.

5. Start working on leadership possibilities—drivers. One leader per car is the logical amount. Have at least one woman/or at least one man. In other words, find driver-leaders of both sexes.

6. As you are receiving answers to your letters, start rounding out the schedule. Picture the trip. Do you have some fun things to do and see? Is your lodging confirmed? If you can swing it, stay at a motel one night. Your drivers can use a comfortable rest.

7. Figure out the cost—excluding meals on the road. This is your fee. Perhaps the church can kick in some money to lower the cost for the youth. Estimate meal costs, so that you can suggest an amount for "spending money."

8. Hopefully, you will know your schedule early. Then, you can publicize with all the information. You probably won't have to do much publicity. It's not hard to get junior highs to go on caravans.

9. Write letters to confirm appointments on the schedule.

10. Start registrations three weeks ahead. Close when full, or at least three days before. Plan to take four or five persons per car.

11. Plan to contact the parents and fully explain the caravan. You could invite parents to one of your meetings. Make it a fun night. Write a letter to all parents. Or, make phone calls.

The parents will need to sign a release form, in case of accident or injury. The following is a sample of such a form:

TO WHOM IT MAY CONCERN
This letter will verify that my child is traveling with (names of drivers), _____, and _____ with my permission. Further, I appoint them, or any of them, my true and lawful agent and attorney-in-fact to consent for me to the obtaining of any and all reasonably necessary medical or surgical treatment.

Signed _____
Parent of

Date _____

_____
Child

12. Write a letter to the youth caravaners, explaining what to bring. Include the schedule. (A sample letter is shown below.)

Dear Caravaner:

We're ready to roll. This is your poop sheet with all the information you'll need on times, money, clothing. We're including phone numbers of our accommodations for you to leave with your parents.

SCHEDULE:

THURSDAY—June 8—Leave Pulaski Heights Presbyterian Church parking lot at 8:15 A.M. You'll need money for lunch and supper on the road.
Sleep—Central Presbyterian Church, Atlanta, on floor.
FRIDAY—June 9:
   9:00 A.M.—Tour of Presbyterian Center
   11:30 A.M.—Meet with Bob Rhea, associate at Central for lunch. Central Church is unique in its ministry to the city of Atlanta. Need money for lunch.
   2:00 P.M.—Meet with Rev. John McRae, director of Aurora, ministry with the counter-culture.
   5:00 P.M.—Six Flags Over Georgia. Admission covered by your church. Need money for supper.
   10:00 P.M.—Underground Atlanta. May wish to have extra spending money here.
Sleep—Central Church.
SATURDAY—June 10:
Sleep late! Lunch on the road to Asheville, North Carolina.
Arrive Asheville before supper; swim time; relax.
Supper at the Bavarian Cellar (this is your best meal—cost approximately $3.50)
We may have the evening free for a movie, so include extra spending.
Sleep—Ramada Inn, Highway 70, East, 704–254–7451
SUNDAY—June 11:
Breakfast.
   11:00 A.M.—Worship at Montreat. This is the opening worship of the General Assembly which is the highest court governing the Presbyterian Church.
Lunch at Montreat.
   2:00 P.M.—Attend General Assembly, with election of moderator. This is especially exciting for us Little Rockians since Dr. Joe Norton of Westover Hills is among the four candidates.
   5:00 P.M.—Leave for Nashville, Tenn. Supper on the road. Sleep—Second Presbyterian Church, Nashville, Tenn.
MONDAY—June 12:
   9:30 a.m.—Meet with representative of the Board of World Missions of our church. Following our meeting we pack up and head for Little Rock. Lunch and supper on the road.
PLEASE READ CAREFULLY!!
COST: Your fee for the trip is $10.00, which we need to have paid on Thursday morning when you arrive at Pulaski Heights.
You can figure about how much you need for meals by the schedule and

your own individual likes. We estimate *$25.00* will fully cover meals. The Ramada Inn room and Six Flags is being covered for you by the three churches.

LUGGAGE: 1 *small* suitcase per person
　　　　　　1 sleeping bag
　　　　　　1 pillow
　　　　　　1 air mattress (optional—floors are hard)
CLOTHING: Shorts, slacks, jeans—comfortable for traveling
　　　　　　One dress outfit—
　　　　　　　　girls: skirt or dress
　　　　　　　　boys: shirt, tie, no coat needed
　　　　　　Swim suit
　　　　　　Towel, soap
PLEASE PACK LIGHT!!
　Again Leave: 8:15 A.M. Thursday, June 8, from Pulaski Heights
　Arrive Home: 7:30 P.M. Monday, June 12, Pulaski Heights parking lot
PHONE NUMBERS FOR PARENTS:
　1. Central Presbyterian Church (Thursday and Friday)—
　　207 Washington Avenue
　　Atlanta, Georgia
　　404–659–0274
　2. Ramada Inn (Saturday)—
　　Highway 70, East
　　Asheville, North Carolina
　　704–254–7451
　3. Second Presbyterian Church (Sunday)—
　　Belmont Blvd.
　　Nashville, Tenn.
　　615–292–2462
Any questions, call:
　Ginny　664–6194
　Jim　　663–8361
Drivers will be:
　Jim Holderness
　Ginny Holderness
　Bob Politzer

You're Off

Before you take off, make sure everyone understands the ground rules:

> Everyone is responsible for his own participation, which means that everyone is to participate in all the activities. No one is to wander off by himself.
> No changes in the car occupancy arrangements. These are the small groups. By changing around often, everyone gets to know everybody very well.

About the Small Groups

The leaders should meet ahead and go over the group building suggestions for use in the cars. Open-ended statements are excellent for facilitating conversation. See Section B, p. 66.

You can use some of the time in the cars for discussing reactions to the projects you are visiting. The leaders should be checking with each other about the discussions in the car.

A worship celebration could be planned for one late evening on the trip.

After the trip, plan to get the caravaners together periodically. They will become very close during the caravan. It could be the start of an active group of youth in your church.

6

Methods

Methods. Some might call them your "bag of tricks." Actually, methods are the means by which you reach your goals. Everything you do with the youth can be called methods—from the serious Bible study to the games and recreation "goodies."

This section includes a variety of methods, all which have been used with junior highs. Some may be familiar. Some may not.

A. GROUP BUILDERS

Group building has to come first. If you look through the window at a junior high meeting on a Sunday night at some church, what you see may look like a "group." But, a gathering of people is not necessarily a *group*. That gathering could meet every Sunday night and still never become a group. So, what is a group?

A GROUP IS A GATHERING OF PEOPLE WHO:

(a) know each other (or at least are in the process of getting to know one another better)
(b) share themselves with the others
(c) care about each other
(d) work together for common purposes

A group, by that definition, doesn't just happen. It takes time. It takes patience. And, it takes a little know-how in group building.

Before describing any techniques, I would like to point you toward the master group builder, Lyman Coleman. He has created hundreds of techniques for building and maintaining groups. Many of his exercises can be found in his section, "Ideas for Groups," in the *Faith at Work* magazine. He is the author of the Serendipity series (*Groups in Action, Acts Alive, Celebration, Discovery, Breaking Free,* and more), which are mini-courses in various aspects of self-discovery and group dynamics. These mini-courses are designed for ninth grade and up, but many of the get-acquainted activities are excellent for junior highs.

The basic elements in group building are:

(1) *Getting Acquainted*—me finding out about you; you finding out about me. Here is where you use ice breakers—something to get the youth talking to each other, loosening up, laughing. Some ice breakers are just fun games, while some give you information about each other.

(2) *Getting Acquainted for Real*—In this stage, each person relates more about himself—facts and feelings about his past, interests and attitudes of his present, and dreams and plans for the future.

(3) *Caring and Affirming*—A group needs to be given opportunities to care about each other. Hopefully, individuals will feel comfortable enough to talk about their concerns. Exercises in which group members affirm each other help build a group. Junior highs need to be accepted. A youth group in which they are affirmed could make the difference in their relationship to the church.

(4) *Working Together*—This is what you are hoping for. A group which shares and cares will enjoy getting together. Call it fellowship. Whatever it is, it is what makes them enjoy youth group. And, this is when they start working together. This is when you see them reach out and give of themselves to the rest of the church and to the community.

This is also when worship becomes a significant experience. Faith doesn't have to be between "me and God." The junior high can know communion, and group building enables communion. It enables community—a need for each other.

The following are games and exercises for group building. *Note:* You, as leader, should participate with your group in all these exercises.

GETTING ACQUAINTED

1. *Simple Introductions*

Instead of the familiar "State your name, age, and school," have everyone introduce himself by stating:

> name
> school
> favorite food
> favorite TV show

You could use:

> favorite singing group
> favorite restaurant
> favorite animal

Think of more!

When to use: when you don't have time for longer "get acquainted" games. At the beginning of the second or third meeting, or any meeting when you have a few new faces.

2. *The Introduction Interview*

A favorite of mine. Pass out paper and pencils to everyone. Have each person get together with someone he does not know (or know very well). Everyone should have a partner.

Instructions: You are to interview your partner—find out as much as you can about him in six minutes—where he was born, favorite food, hobby, TV show, likes, dislikes—whatever you would like to ask him. Jot all this down on paper.

Obviously, you are to be interviewing each other at the same time. Keep firing questions at each other and writing down information.

After six or seven minutes, call time. Have everyone gather in one group if you have fourteen or less people. If you have more, split into groups of eight to ten each. Ask someone to start by introducing to the group the person he interviewed. Go around the circle until everyone has been introduced.

When to use:

    the first meeting
    the first exercise at a retreat
    when you are having a special event with other youth groups

Materials: paper and pencils

3. *Descriptive Name Tags*

Have all members of the group take a piece of construction paper (at least (6″ x 10″) and a felt pen. They are to write their names across the top in large letters. Then, have them write four or five words describing themselves (their interests, attributes). However, the words must end in "ing" or "able." For example: guitar-playing, tennisable, carefreeing. The words need not be real words, but they must have "ing" or "able" tacked on the end. They should write these words anywhere on the paper on the same side as their names. Have them pin on their name tags or wear them with string hanging around their necks.

Now, they are to roam around the room, reading everyone's name tag, asking questions if they like.

The rule is: THEY ARE TO MAKE SURE THEY READ EVERY TAG. One additional rule might be—they are to touch every single person in the room with one finger. This is a little silly, but they like it. It does guarantee that no one is left out.

When to use:

first meeting
when there are several new faces
at an event with other youth groups

Materials:

construction paper
felt pens
pins

4. Name Tag Symbols [2]

Have all members of the group take a piece of paper. They are to think of four interests they have, four things that are very important to them at the present. Draw a symbol for each of the four on the name tag paper. They should also put their names somewhere on the paper. Have them pin on the name tags. When everyone has finished, have each person describe his name tag to the group. If your group is larger than fourteen, split into two or more groups.

When to use:

first meeting
when there are several new faces
at an event with other youth groups

Materials:

paper
pencils
pins

5. Name Tag Collage [3]

This exercise is similar to number 4, except that it allows some creativity in preparing a mini-collage.

As individuals arrive, explain that they are to make a name tag collage. They are to cut a piece of construction paper in any shape they wish. Then, direct them to piles of magazines, newspapers, and glue. They are to find five or six pictures or words that would tell something about "who they are." After they have finished, they should put a string through it and wear it around their necks.

When everyone has finished, have each person introduce himself to the group by describing his collage.

When to use:

same as in number 4—when you have a little more time at your disposal

Materials:

construction paper
magazines and newspapers

glue
string
felt pens, regular pens
scissors

6. *John, John, John*

This is an exercise for review of names. The leader stands in the middle of the circle. Everyone is seated on the floor or in chairs. The leader explains that he will flip around the circle, pointing at different people. When he points, everyone is to say that person's name in a resounding chorus. When a name comes a little slowly to the group, stand over that person and point, point, point, point, until everyone is saying: "Fred, Fred, Fred, Fred" with assurance. For fun, keep going back to one person.

When to use:

any time—you want to make sure that everyone knows everybody

7. *Can't Say "No!"*

This game is more of an ice breaker than a "get acquainted" exercise.

Everyone is given ten beans. The object is to take beans from persons by getting them to say "no," "nothing," "uh-uh," "never." Tell everyone to mill around the room asking questions of each other. They can be questions about anything, hopefully about something for which they will receive a negative response.

Each time an individual gets someone to say "no" or something negative, he takes one of their beans. Allow the game to go on for ten minutes. The person with the most beans wins. (The prize is up to you.)

When to use:

as part of an informal get acquainted time during a special event
when you're having a large crowd

Materials:

a bag of beans

GETTING ACQUAINTED FOR REAL

8. *Collage on Me*

This is an expansion of exercise 5. The group is given thirty minutes to look through magazines and newspapers and make a collage on who they are—their interests, their values, their likes and dislikes, their hopes and dreams. The collage should be made on full size posterboard (22″ x 28″). After everyone has finished, each person should explain his collage to the group. Use smaller groupings, if you have more than twelve people.

When to use:

at a first meeting
at a retreat

Materials:

posterboard
magazines and newspapers
glue
scissors

9. *Open-Ended Statements*

Open-ended statements are sentence stems which are to be finished by each individual. Example: On Saturdays, I like to . . . The leader states the sentence stem and then, goes around the circle, letting each person finish the sentence. This is done quickly. Usually there is no discussion.
When to use:

for getting acquainted
for an opinion survey
for any occasion

You can make up open-ended statements for any purpose. If you are exploring values, make up value-related stems. Use in a Bible study, such as:

If I had been in Peter's shoes, I would have . . .
Faith is . . .

Use the following for getting acquainted:

If I could have lunch with a famous person, it would be . . .
If I had $25,000 to give away, I would . . .
If I could go anywhere in the world and live for three months, I would go to . . .

10. *Think of*

Use the following as you would the open-ended statements:
Think of an animal that would describe who you are.
Think of three silly fears you had as a child.
Think of three crazy dreams you had as a child of what you wanted to be or do when you grew up. (You will find that some aren't so crazy. One girl may say she wanted to be a doctor, and still does.)
Think of three big disappointments you had as a child. (They can be little things or big disappointments. Many which seem little now were big then.)
THINK OF MORE!

11. *Two Adjectives* [4]

Pass out paper and pencils. Ask each person to think a minute and write down two adjectives he would use to describe himself. Then, ask them to think of two adjectives their parents would use to describe them. Write these down, and then, two adjectives their friends would use.

Go around the circle, having each share his answers.

12. *In Event of Fire* [5]

This exercise concerns what one values in life. Tell the group to imagine that each of their houses is on fire and they have only three minutes to save their most valuable possessions.

What four things (other than people) would you try to save? Go around the circle, letting each person list his four items. Ask them to explain why they chose those particular items.

13. *Guess Who?* [6]

This group builder is a game which gives more information about individuals. It is best played in a group which has been together for a while.

Pass out slips of paper and pencils and a 3″ x 5″ card. Have each person put his answers to the following questions on his slip of paper:

1. Where were you born?
2. Where is the farthest place you have ever visited?
3. What is your favorite song?
4. The thing I wanted to be when I was a child . . .

After everyone has finished, collect the slips. You are going to read a slip, Number 1. They are to guess who they think wrote that slip and write that name on their card for Number 1. Then, read the second slip, and so forth.

After you have read them all, go back to Number 1, read it again, and ask who they put down. After the shouting of names, ask the person who did write it to confess. How many were right?

CARING AND AFFIRMING

14. *Virginia Reel Conversation*

This is a fun way to encourage listening on a one-to-one basis. Have everyone line up Virginia Reel style—two lines of equal length. Sit on the floor (or in chairs) with lines facing each other, a foot apart.

You have a list of questions or open-ended statements (see exercise 9). Ask the first question. The pairs have two or three minutes to talk with each other about that question, each giving the other his answer.

Call time. Only one line moves. That line moves to the left one person.

The end person comes down and fills the empty space at the other end. Each person has a new conversation partner. The leader reads the next question. Again, each person talks with the person in front of him for two or three minutes. Time is called. The line moves to the left again, and so on.

Remind the youth that they are conversing. The following questions are samples of those which might be used Virginia Reel style:

1. How can people make you angry?
2. What is the most significant thing that happened to you this week?
3. What is the silliest gift you ever received for Christmas?
4. What is something you worry about?
5. What would you like to change about yourself?
6. What adult has greatly influenced your life?
7. What is something you are afraid of?
8. What is important to you in a friendship?
9. Where would you like to live, other than your present location?
10. What is your favorite thing to do on a vacation?

15. *Color Me* [7]

As the group members get to know each other, this exercise will give them an opportunity to think about each person in the group. Do this in small groups of six to eight people.

Instructions: You are to think of a color for each person in the group, a color which describes him. First, pick a person to be the first subject. He remains silent, while each person names a color he has chosen for the subject and explains why he gave him that color.

After everyone has given him a color, the subject should say what color he would give himself.

The exercise continues with each person having a chance to be the subject.

THE FOLLOWING THREE ARE THE BEST I HAVE SEEN FOR AFFIRMATION. They should be used after the junior highs have been together for a while, and are excellent for retreats and conferences. All three are adapted from Lyman Coleman.

16. *Strength Bombardment* [8]

This exercise provides a chance for each person to receive praise, encouragement, and good feelings from the members of the group.

Arrange the chairs in the shape of a horseshoe. Place an empty chair at the open end. One at a time each person in the group will sit quietly in the chair and be bombarded with affirmations. Go around the circle, having each person say something he likes about the person. For example, "I really like your sense of humor," or "You say what you think. I admire that." AFFIRMATIONS ONLY! Not negative comments.

Each person should have a turn at being affirmed.

When to use:

> any time during the year; watch for signs of group cohesiveness when junior highs are enjoying each other
> as a group
> as part of a worship experience

17. Gift-Giving—Symbolic [9]

This exercise enables the group members to express positive feelings toward one another by giving gifts. The gifts are objects, such as things one would find in one's purse or wallet, an object found in the room or outdoors, or something one could make (out of paper, wire, or clay). The gifts are symbolic of feelings toward the other persons. Many, such as keys, may need to be returned at the end of the session.

The participants will need time to think about each person in their group and to find the gifts. If your group is large, divide them into smaller groups of six to eight persons each.

When the group assembles after finding their gifts, ask someone to start off by giving out his gifts and explaining the symbolism for each. Then, the next person gives out all his gifts, etc.

18. Gift-Giving—Emotional [10]

Instruct the group to think of the greatest gifts they could give to the others in terms of human emotions or character traits. For example:

> "Jan, I give you the gift of patience, so that you won't get so upset with your parents."
> "Don, I give you the gift of caring, because you said that you really wished you could care about other people."

The procedure is similar to the Strength Bombardment procedure. Have one person remain silent, while the others each give him their gifts. Each person is to have a turn at receiving.

When to use:

> both gift-giving exercises are excellent for use at retreats and conferences in small groups of six to eight people
> as part of a worship experience

19. Prayer

There are many ways prayer can be meaningful to a group of junior highs. At the same time, praying out loud can be an embarrassing experience. It takes sensitivity and a little imagination to find appropriate ways to pray together.

At some point, ask your junior highs about prayer. Have them relate meaningful experiences in other groups. Ask them for suggestions.

CELEBRATION!   CELEBRATION!   CELEBRATION!

As worship is celebration, prayer can be celebration. Sing in a circle. Lock arms or get in a football huddle. You lead in prayer. At times, individuals can lead in prayer. When praying out loud in a group, suggest that two or three pray and you will close. Then, everyone will shout "AMEN!" Avoid going around the circle in order because each person is put on the spot and it is hard to actually pray.

Prayers can be written ahead of time and offered by one person. Small groups can write prayers. Have one person from each group read the prayer. After each, have the group say: "Hear our prayer, O Lord," or "We praise you, Lord!"

B. VALUES CLARIFICATION

If anyone asked me to name the most effective method I have recently used with junior highs, I would probably say: VALUES CLARIFICATION. It's not "The Answer" to all your problems. However, it is a method which you may find helpful, and it could be a vital part of your program. I suggest that you check the resources and do some reading about it.

VALUES CLARIFICATION IS A PROCESS by which one discovers what is important to him, and examines his own behavior in light of what he values.

The world offers junior highs conflicting values. From parents they receive one set of values, from friends another, from school another, from church another, from the president another, from television another, and on and on.

They are constantly faced with decisions—for now and for the future. How do they make decisions? How do they sort out the input they receive from so many value sources? How do they know which values, attitudes, and beliefs are their own?

Values clarification is a systematic approach to help persons think through value issues. The approach was formulated by Louis Raths, co-author of *Values and Teaching*. He breaks down the process of valuing into seven sub-processes: [11]

CHOOSING:	(1) freely
	(2) from alternatives
	(3) after thoughtful consideration of the consequences of each alternative
PRIZING:	(4) cherishing, being happy with the choice
	(5) willing to affirm the choice publicly

ACTING: (6) doing something with the choice
              (7) repeatedly, in some pattern of life

These seven sub-processes serve as criteria by which one can judge his own beliefs and behavior patterns. For example, you might say that you value equality for all men. Ask yourself the following questions: [12]

1. Did you consider the alternatives in choosing your position?
2. Have you carefully considered the consequences of the alternatives and of your position?
3. Do you feel it was you own choice, your own position, or were you highly influenced by other persons?
4. Are you happy with your position or belief? Proud of it?
5. Are you willing to affirm your position publicly? Have you ever?
6. Do you act on your position? Does your belief determine the way you act?
7. Do you act on your position repeatedly? Has it become a part of your pattern of life?

If you said "yes" to all seven, then equality for all men is truly part of your value system, part of your values.

If you said "no" to any question, then you now know what you need to do to make "equality for all men" an important principle in your life.

The exercises in values clarification are fun which junior highs really enjoy doing. They are given opportunities to think through issues and to speak out their opinions. Everyone gets a chance to speak, to participate. No one is put down for his ideas or left out.

Sounds great, right? So, where do you get these exercises? There are two mini-courses on values in Section C with suggested exercises. (See "Value Process," p. 103, and "Values: Theirs, Mine, and Ours," p. 121.)

However, the best place to find exercises is in *Values Clarification: A Handbook of Practical Strategies for Teachers and Students* by Sidney B. Simon, Leland W. Howe, and Howard Kirschenbaum.

There are several other books, cassettes, and kits dealing in values clarification, some of which are given in the resource list below.

When to use:

as mini-courses in valuing, such as those given in Section C, p. 103 and p. 121
to introduce certain subjects; many of the exercises, such as A Question of Priority (p. 105), the Interview (p. 114) and Voting (p. 111), can be used for opinion-gathering
in Bible study and Christian ethics to elicit individual's feelings and attitudes

Note: Values clarification came along at the right time for youth groups. Have any of you experienced the frustration of trying to discuss a topic? You ask "What do you think about . . . ?" or "What is your own personal feeling on . . . ?" And, you get blank stares, silence, or "I dunno."

The structured exercises in values clarification can get you out of that slump.

RESOURCES

Values Clarification: A Handbook of Practical Strategies for Teachers and Students, by Simon, Howe, and Kirschenbaum. (Hart Pub. Co.)
   79 exercises in Values Clarification.
Values and Teaching by Louis E. Raths, Merrill Harmin, and Sidney B. Simon. (Charles E. Merrill Publishing Co.)
   Describes the theory behind Values Clarification.
A Workshop on Values Clarification, Teacher/Leader Training Unit 8. (Seabury Press.)
   Teaches the process of valuing.
Values Systems Techniques
   a 16mm film, 28 minutes, black and white. Available from the Audiovisual Library of the Episcopal Church. Rental $8.
The following are available from Argus Communications, 7440 Natchez Avenue, Niles, Illinois 60648.
Meeting Yourself Halfway by Sidney B. Simon.
   31 strategies for self-discovery
   book—paperback $4.95
   kit—18.50 (Jr./Sr. High–Adult)
Making Sense of Our Lives by Merrill Harmin.
   kit for junior and senior highs
   cassettes
   posters
   value sheets
Strike It Rich
   filmstrip and record/cassette
   8 minutes
The IALAC Story (I Am Lovable and Capable)
   pamphlet and filmstrip
You Have to Want Something
   filmstrip and record/cassette

C. A LITTLE CREATIVITY

Junior highs vary in their enthusiasm over creative activities. Some will spend hours making posters and banners. Others will swear they can't do anything. I am always on the look out for new ideas in this area and here am describing only a few.

1. *Collage*

A collage is a pièce d'art made out of magazines and/or newspaper clippings, words, and pictures placed in random form all over a posterboard. Three-dimensional objects can also be used.

Collages usually have a theme. A collage can be an expression of art on:

Me
The Church
People
Giving
Love
Hope

It can represent any issue. A group of seventh graders once made a collage describing their minister and presented it to him, as he was leaving that church for a different position.

When to use:

in connection with any topic
for getting acquainted
on retreats, church-ins, special events

Caution: You can overuse collages.

Materials:

posterboard
magazines and newspapers
construction paper
felt pens
glue
scissors
any three-dimensional objects, like cloth, foil, cotton

2. *Banners*

Banners are usually made on large pieces of felt, burlap, or some similar cloth. Words and symbols can be cut out of the same materials and glued on the large piece with glue.

Pieces of wood, called dowels, can be placed in a hem at the top. String is then attached to the wood. And, the banner hangs.

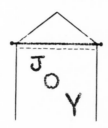

When to use:

in worship, banners can be an effective aid to celebration

Banners can express themes of the Christian faith—Love, Joy, Faith, Hope. Ideas for banners can be found in catalogues of posters.

Materials:

cloth—felt, burlap, cotton
felt pieces
wooden dowels (check at a lumber supply store or a hobby shop)
scissors
string or cord
glue

3. *Posters*

Posters can be made on posterboard or paper. They can be plain, fancy, symbolic. Printing and drawings can be made with felt pens or tempera paint. Symbols and letters can be made out of construction paper and glued on.

When to use:

for publicity—to advertise your meetings, retreats, and special events
Example: for a car caravan, posters were made on which were glued sections of road maps.
for mini-courses, topics, issues, as a means to express feelings about the topic or to communicate facts
for use in displays; use for a presentation of a topic to a church school class

Materials:

posterboard or paper
felt pens, tempera paint
construction paper
various other materials for gluing
scissors
glue
pencils

4. *Murals*

A mural is a series of pictures or some form of art on a long sheet of butcher paper. Murals can tell a story or describe different parts of a topic being studied.

Or, a mural can be a collection of graffiti—words, sentences expressing feelings.

When to use:

for storytelling—on a particular subject
For example, you might be rephrasing a Scripture passage in a modern-day setting. After it is written, each person could take a section of the

mural and draw a part of the modern day story. The art work can be very impressionistic.

During a retreat or special event—Have a large sheet of butcher paper stretched out on a table or wall. Tell the group it is a graffiti sheet. Have them write something in response to the theme of the retreat. They can write on it at any time.

Materials:

a roll of butcher paper
felt pens or crayons

5. Clay

Clay is such a versatile art material. It can be used in group building exercises for expresing feelings. In mini-courses on identity and relationships, the junior highs could make clay sculptures representing:

Fear	Joy
Anger	Alienation
Conflict	Reconciliation
Love	Peace

In worship, clay expressions can be molded as part of the celebration. Small groups can put their lumps of clay together and form a group expression.

When to use:

for mini-courses, retreats, special events
for personal and group expressions
for worship

Materials:

modeling clay
oil cloth (to cover the modeling area)
paper towels

6. Wire Sculpture

Use for the same purposes as clay. Almost any kind of wire can be used—copper wire, aluminum wire, etc. As with the clay sculptures, have each person explain his sculpture to the group.

Materials:

aluminum or copper wire
wire cutters

7. Mobiles

Mobiles require a little imagination and a sense of balance. A mobile is composed of coat hanger sections, strings, and objects (symbols) which hang. Getting the strings tied on to the hanger bars in the proper place for balance is the trick.

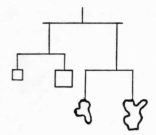

Materials:

   coat hangers
   wire cutters
   scissors
   string
   glue
   tape
   objects: construction paper, aluminum foil, styrofoam, any objects.

D. WITH PAPER AND PENCIL

Many youth leaders shy away from any form of writing activity, for fear of it being "too much like school." There are several ways of using paper and pencil that can be fun. Some are very simple, some very creative.

1. Interviews

This method was described in the "getting acquainted" section of Group Builders (exercise 2, p. 63). It's an example of simple use of paper and pencil. The participants are to write down facts about the person they interview. This exercise is a good way to break the ice for writing things down, after which it will be easier for them to write down thoughts and opinions in other activities.

2. Valuing Exercises

Check the valuing exercises used in the values mini-courses, p. 103 & p. 121. In these, the youth fill out charts and write down alternatives. Again, these are simple writing exercises.

3. Paraphrasing and Rewriting

In Bible studies, you can find opportunities for creativity through paraphrasing and rewriting.

Paraphrasing is the rewriting of a passage without using any of the same words (exceptions are made for small words, i.e., of, and, in, the).

Example: Romans 12:4–5 (RSV)

For as in one body we have many members, and all the members do not have the same function, so we, though many, are one body in Christ, and individually members one of another.

Paraphrase:

If you look at me physically, you see that I have eyes, mouth, ears, hands, etc., many parts. And, they all serve a different purpose. It is the same in the church. Each of us has a unique purpose. But, we are "one in the Spirit." We are a community. We all are needed. We all work together.

Rewriting is the taking of a Bible passage and writing it in a modern day setting. This is excellent for passages with story lines.

Example: Luke 15:3–7 The Parable of the Lost Sheep (RSV)

So he told them this parable: "What man of you, having a hundred sheep, if he has lost one of them, does not leave the ninety-nine in the wilderness, and go after the one which is lost, until he finds it? And when he has found it, he lays it on his shoulders, rejoicing. And when he comes home, he calls together his friends and his neighbors, saying to them, 'Rejoice with me, for I have found my sheep which was lost.' Even so, I tell you, there will be more joy in heaven over one sinner who repents than over ninety-nine righteous persons who need no repentance."

Rewriting in modern day setting:

A bus driver was taking a group of five-year-olds to the zoo. They followed him all the way, seeing all the fascinating animals. At the day's end, they all climbed on the bus to go home. The bus driver counted them. One little boy was missing. The zoo was closing. The bus driver leaped off the bus and ran through the closing gate. He hunted and searched. The zoo was so big. He went past the lions, the birds, the elephants, and the monkeys. No sign of the little boy.

And finally, on the sidewalk by the polar bear's pool, sat the lost boy, crying. The bus driver bent over and boosted him up high on his shoulders. The bus driver was so joyful over finding the lost boy. He ran to the bus, where the rest of the children were waiting. They all cheered. The bus driver bought popcorn and balloons for everyone. They all celebrated, for the lost little boy was found.

This story is an adaptation of an excellent 14 minute film, THE STRAY, from TeleKETICS.

For passages which convey teachings, as in Paul's letters, the youth would think up a modern situation and rewrite the teachings in words that would apply. They might write a letter to their church.

Sometimes the youth will react negatively, saying they just can't think of anything. That's one reason why it is best to use this technique in small groups—very small groups. Have three or four work together on a paraphrase. You'll be surprised with what they can do.

Allow the groups twenty minutes to work on a passage. With everyone together, have someone from each group read their paraphrase or modern day setting.

4. *Newspaper Reports*

Another creative writing method for use in Bible study is the newspaper report. Taking a story from a passage or a teaching, the youth would act as reporters and write the story for a front page scoop. Like the paraphrase, this is more effective when you use small groups—three or four working together.
Example: Taken from Matthew 8:23–27

STRANGE PHENOMENON ON THE SEA OF GALILEE

A most unusual event occurred on the Sea of Galilee yesterday afternoon about 3:45 P.M. In the midst of the sunny, balmy weather we've been having for the last two weeks, a severe storm appeared on the lake. Disaster seemed imminent for all fishing boats. However, in one of the boats was the teacher Jesus, who has been causing quite a stir in our countryside.

One of the fishermen, whose name shall be withheld, told UPN news reporters that this Jesus stood up in the tossing boat and spoke harshly to the winds and the sea. AND, THE STORM CEASED IMMEDIATELY! The fisherman reported: "Our boat was being swamped. We were going to drown. The Master was asleep. We woke him. We were so afraid. He acted like nothing was wrong. He stood up and commanded the storm to stop. And, it did! Immediately!"

People all over Galilee are talking about this man. Who is he? The winds and the sea obey him. No one seems to be able to explain the calming of the sea.

5. *Scripts*

Small groups can work out scripts for:

dramatizing a Bible passage
dramatizing an issue
for a role play
    or
for slide or movie productions.

In a drama script, the youth would write a story telling what each person says. A script for slides or movies can be a collection of sayings, poetry, or Scripture. Or, it can be a description of the slides.

6. *Self-Contracts*

Self-contracts, obviously, are not written by groups. This is an individual technique. A self-contract is a statement you make with yourself about something you intend to do or some change you intend to make in your life.

This technique is used toward the end of mini-courses or discussions, when the youth are reflecting on various issues which affect them personally.

If they really intend to carry out their contracts, they sign their names at the bottom. A week later you can take time to talk about the contracts. How is everybody doing? What problems are they having?

7. Newsprint Stems

Happiness is . . .
School is . . .
Commitment is . . .
I can't stand . . .
Love is . . .
Church is . . .
I like . . .

These are sentence stems which can be printed at the top of a newsprint sheet. During a meeting or event, the sheet is hung in a place where the youth can write their feelings and ideas, completing the statement.

This is a good technique for beginning a session. Direct the youth to the sheet as they are arriving. The sentence stem should deal with the topic of the session. Or, if you are having a fun night or recreation, have several newsprint stems displayed. Use fun stems, like:

Peanut butter is . . .
My next door neighbor . . .
Christmas is . . .
I love to . . .

It is a good way to find out your junior high's opinions on various issues.

8. Cinquain

Now we are getting to some real creativity. A CINQUAIN (pronounced sin-can′) is a French poetry form, consisting of five lines. Its composition follows these guidelines:

Line 1: Title (a noun; one word)
Line 2: Describes the title (two words)
Line 3: Action words or phrase about the title (three words)
Line 4: Describes a feeling about the title (four words)
Line 5: Refers to the title (one word)

Example of a cinquain on "Freedom" would be:

Freedom
Come alive
To be me
No more guilt feelings
Release

A cinquain on "God":

God
Loving Father
Forgiving all men
My reason for being
Love

Cinquains can be written on any subject. If you wish, you can give the junior highs the first line or title.

9. Haiku

A HAIKU (pronunced hi'-koo) is a Japanese art form, consisting of three lines. The first line consists of five syllables, the second of seven, and the third five.

The following is an example of a haiku on "God":

The Giver of life
Has sent his Son for us all
And desires our love.

E. SIGHTS 'N' SOUNDS

There is such a variety of ways to use slides, movies, cameras, records, and tape players. And, there are many catalogues and books available on using audio-visuals. I shall merely mention a few suggestions.

1. Slides

The best advice on slides is to *collect them*. Keep a file. There are excellent slides available on all kinds of subjects. Youth can put together slide productions on any topic. They write their own scripts. Or, they could make a tape recording of words and music to accompany the slides.

In worship, slides can be used with:

call to worship
prayers
the Word—Scripture and the proclamation (a twenty minute presentation in place of a sermon)
hymns (words to hymns may be put on slides)
as part of communion—to interpret the meaning of the Lord's Supper
as part of the offertory

There are innumerable possibilities for creativity in worship.

The following are sets of slides.

MARK IV (two sets)
Available from MARK IV
La Salette Center
Attleboro, Massachusetts 02703

TeleSLIDES
  Available from Franciscan Communications Center
                1229 South Santee Street
                Los Angeles, California 90015

Discovery in Slides
  Available from Paulist Press
                400 Sette Drive
                Paramus, N. J. 07652

Probing the World
  Available from Paulist Press
                400 Sette Drive
                Paramus, N. J. 07652

Visual and Verbal Meditations
  Available from New Life Films
                Box 2008
                Kansas City, Kansas 66110

2. *Make Your Own Slides*

It is possible to make your own slides, that is, slides which you can write on or color with felt pens. You will need acetate and slide mounts. The acetate may be purchased in large sheets or rolls from a hobby shop. The slide mounts are the cardboard frames (2" x 2"), which you can get at a camera store.

Cut the acetate into little squares, small enough to be inserted into the frames. Some mounts need to be sealed with an iron. You then have a slide.

You can color the slide with felt pens and scratch out words with a tooth pick. Such slides produce interesting effects when used with music and readings.

Did you ever wonder if it were possible to make slides from a picture in a book or magazine? It is. However, you need an Ektagraphic Visual Maker. This is a kit which includes a Kodak Instamatic camera, copy-stands, close-up lenses, film, flashcubes, and batteries. It is quite complete. And, it is quite expensive, costing perhaps $110. So, if you are interested in making slides from pictures, which will provide you with permanent slide resources, see if you can borrow one. Or, you might suggest to your church school budget person that your church needs to consider purchasing one.

An excellent resource, which describes the materials and processes for making slides (and films) is the *Slide and Film Making Manual* by Donald Griggs. It is available from: Griggs Educational Service, P.O. Box 362,

Livermore, California 94550. Griggs also distributes a Film and Slide Making Kit, which contains everything you would need for a project in either slide of film production.

3. Filmstrips

Filmstrips are growing in popularity. Many books have their own filmstrips for use in classrooms and with youth groups. One example is *Why Am I Afraid to Tell You Who I Am?* by John Powell (filmstrip produced by Argus Communications).

It is possible to have a filmstrip made from slides. It is quite expensive, like a dollar per slide. But, your group may be working on a production over a period of weeks, and you may feel it's worth preserving. In this case you can ask your local photo store to have your slides made into a filmstrip. This is a good idea, especially if your production has to do with the life of the church, the mission of your church, or a special study which could be used in the future.

A script will have to be prepared for the filmstrip. Or, your group might make a tape recording by putting together music from recordings and/or live music, and words, readings, etc.

Another method with filmstrips is to cut up a filmstrip and make slides, using the 2″ x 2″ slide mounts which were described in "Make your own slides." This gives you a number of slides which can be used over and over again in a variety of productions.

4. Movies

(a) 16mm movies are for fun, thought, and discussion.

Fun—From W. C. Fields, *The Hunchback of Notre Dame,* and the Three Stooges to many of the modern day films, you can find hundreds of films available at fairly reasonable rentals. "Movie nights" are great social events for junior highs. Make some popcorn. Let them invite their friends. And, have a couple of movies.

Write to the following companies for catalogues:

        Macmillan Audio Brandon
        34 MacQuesten Parkway So.
        Mount Vernon, N. Y. 10550

        Films Incorporated
        4420 Oakton Street
        Skokie, Illinois 60076

Thought and discussion—Some movies are thought provoking and thus hard to discuss. You will want to use these in worship or as part of a study. Others are made for discussion. In fact, many include a sheet of discussion

questions. Most of the movies I have used have either been INSIGHT
FILMS, produced by
>Paulist Productions
>P.O. Box 1057
>Pacific Palisades, California 90272

or TeleKETICS Films, produced by
>Franciscan Communications Center
>1229 South Santee Street
>Los Angeles, California 90015

Another possibility is:
>Mass Media
>2116 N. Charles Street
>Baltimore, Maryland 21218

An excellent catalog for media resources is *The Audio-Visual Resource Guide,* edited by Nick Abrams (Friendship Press, publisher).

Caution: ALWAYS PREVIEW THE FILM. I have had a couple of occasions where I have had to scratch a film because it was inappropriate. And I have also had a few very embarrassing occasions where I did not preview the film, and it bombed miserably.

Another caution: Movies are pretty easy. They take little preparation (except previewing). They are too easy and can be overused. Don't expect movies to make up for lack of ideas or planning.

(b) 8mm and super 8mm are for making your own movies.

Youth love to think up crazy antics and skits to put on film. You could spend hours filming everything they wanted to film. For a fun night, borrow an 8mm or Super 8mm and light—some Super 8's don't need a light. Divide the junior highs into small groups. Have each group think of a series of skits or short funnies for filming. When one group is ready, film it. If you are not familiar with movie cameras, have someone else do the filming.

The best part, of course, is seeing the film after it is developed.

Another idea: Consider making a thirty or sixty second spot like the Cancer Society and other agencies do for television. You could do it as a related activity for a study or mini-course. Or, make several spots with specifically Christian messages.

Make a five or ten minute movie on various activities in your church. Arrange for your junior high photographers to visit classes, meetings, fellowship groups, and fun times.

Make a movie of one of your junior high projects.

Film dramatizations, role plays, tableaux, musical activities.

(c) The Talkie—If anyone in your congregation has a Kodak Ektasound 140—"the Talkie"—movie camera, ask them if they would come to a junior high meeting and do some filming. This is ideal for any dramatic presentation.

(d) Animation—I have never tried making an animated film. But, I know persons who have. It is a creative, fascinating technique. You might check it out. See:

> *Make Your Own Animated Movies* by Yvonne Andersen (Little, Brown and Company).
> *Teaching Film Animation to Children* by Yvonne Andersen (Van Nostrand Reinhold Company).

5. Snapshots

Just having a camera around is a smart idea. One or two junior highs who like to take pictures could be the photographers for the group. In this way you will always have pictures of various activities.

Snapshots can be placed on posters for publicity, or used as a display of a particular subject.

A series of posters on "our group" might have a snapshot of each youth and words or symbols which tell "who he is."

One last word on photography: Don't forget the cameras on retreats, church-ins, trips, and other events. Plan ahead with your youth photographers, so they will know what situations to cover. It seems like you always get too many pictures of one thing and not enough of others. In planning for a retreat or conference, make a list of the pictures you want. You'll need the setting, buildings, signs, people getting on and off buses, people eating. Imagine the final production when you're making your list.

6. Tape Players

Reel-to-reel and cassette recorders are the most useful tape players for youth groups. Each has its advantages.

The reel to reel

> —can be edited. You can splice the tape.
> —has better quality, because it usually has three speeds. The 7½ ips (inches per second) gives the best quality and should be used for taping music.

The cassette

> —is handy. It's small and can be carried around for taping interviews. It can be taken on retreats, trips, and conferences.
> —can be operated on batteries, so you don't have to be near an outlet.

What can you do with tape players?

> —Tape music and readings to accompany slide productions.
> —Tape music for the prelude in a worship service or for background to the Scripture reading.

—Tape "man on the street" interviews. Have a junior high take a cassette recorder to a church school class, where he can interview adults, other youth, or children on a certain topic.

SOUND COLLAGE—a very creative expression. A sound collage is a collection of sounds. It could be music, singing, speaking. It could be laughter, bells, traffic sounds, crying, coughing, electronic sounds, industrial sounds.

Procedure: The group is working on a particular subject. They decide on a theme or message which they'd like to produce in a sixty second, three minute, or five minute sound collage. It may be wise to divide into smaller groups and have each group produce a segment of the collage, or have each smaller group produce its own.

First, they are to make a list of sounds they want to record. They decide on the order. Then, they discuss how they are going to find all these sounds. They should divide up the responsibility. Cassettes can be used in recording. But, for the final product, transfer the cassette segments to reel-to-reel. Then, the splicing begins.

F. MUSIC

1. *Popular Songs*

As a leader, you'll need to listen to the "pop" station on your radio every once in a while to keep up with the music. Keep track of the popular singing groups. Ask the youth to keep you informed.

Listen to the words of these songs. What are they saying? You might have to ask the junior highs for the lyrics. With some songs, it is hard to understand the words. Make note of certain songs which could be used:

for discussion
for worship
for group singing

Some songs of the 60's and 70's have been used for these purposes. You may have heard some in connection with youth work. Examples:

"Bridge Over Troubled Water" (Simon and Garfunkel)
"The Impossible Dream" (*Man of La Mancha*)
"Day by Day" (*Godspell*)
"Prepare Ye the Way of the Lord" (*Godspell*)
"He Ain't Heavy, He's My Brother" (The Hollies)
"Lean on Me" (Bill Withers)
"Morning Has Broken" (Cat Stevens)
"O Happy Day" (Edwin Hawkins Singers)
"The Sounds of Silence" (Simon and Garfunkel)

"I'd Like to Teach the World to Sing" (The Hillside Singers)
"Everything is Beautiful" (Ray Stevens)
"Turn! Turn! Turn!" (Pete Seeger, based on Ecclesiastes)
"You've Got a Friend" (Carole King, recorded by James Taylor)
"Tie a Yellow Ribbon Round the Ole Oak Tree" (Tony Orlando and Dawn)
"I Never Promised You a Rose Garden" (Joe South, recorded by Lynn Anderson)
"One Tin Soldier" (Dennis Lambert and Brian Porter)
"Let It Be" (Lennon and McCartney)

2. *Songs for Group Singing*

Singing is an integral part of youth work. If someone in your group plays guitar, you're in luck. Now all you need is some songs to sing. The following is a list of "standards for youth groups"—songs that most of the junior highs know and like to sing.

"They'll Know We are Christians by Our Love"
"Allelu"
"He's Everything to Me"
"Seek and Ye Shall Find"
"Amen!"
"Day by Day"
"Amazing Grace"
"Morning Has Broken"
"Let Us Break Bread Together"
"His Sheep Am I"
"Kum Ba Yah"
"Blowin' in the Wind"
"This Land"
"Today"
"Pass It On"
"Put Your Hand in the Hand"
"Gonna Sing, My Lord"
"Here We Are"
The "Love" round
"All My Trials"
"Lord of the Dance"
"Shalom"
"O Freedom"
"In Christ There is No East or West"

All of the above can be found in one or more of the following songbooks:

Hymns for Now, edited by R. Paul Firnhaber ($1.00)
Hymns for Now II, edited by R. Paul Firnhaber ($1.00)
 Both available from:
  Concordia Publishing House
  3558 South Jefferson Avenue
  St. Louis, Missouri 63118
Ventures in Song, edited by David J. Randolph
  Abingdon Press
  201 8th Avenue South
  Nashville, Tennessee 37202
Hymnal for Young Christians ($5.00)
 Available from:
  F. E. L. Publications
  22 East Huron
  Chicago, Illinois 60661
Sing 'N' Celebrate!, compiled by Kurt Kaiser, Sonny Salsbury, Billy Ray Hearn ($1.50)
 Available from:
  Word, Inc.
  Box 1790
  Waco, Texas 76703
New Wine: Songs for Celebration, edited by Jim Strathdee and Nelson Stringer ($1.50)
 Available from:
  United Methodist Church Board of Education
  5250 Santa Monica Blvd.
  Los Angeles, California 90029
Song Book for Saints and Sinners, compiled by Carlton R. Young (1–12 copies, $1.00 each; 13 or more copies, $.75 each)
  Agape
  Main Place
  Carol Stream, Illinois 60187

3. *Music in Worship*

(a) Sing hymns and songs with guitar or autoharp.

(b) Have a soloist with guitar sing "Let Us Break Bread Together" during communion. The soloist should be hidden.

(c) Line out a psalm. Lining out could be considered a method of choral reading. A leader speaks a line of the psalm with special feeling—he may shout, or whisper, or stress certain words. He may sing one line, like a chant. The congregation then repeats the words exactly as the leader spoke them. The leader may use clapping or snapping of fingers with certain lines. He may use hand and arm motions. He may stand up on certain lines, and sit down on others. After each, the congregation does the same. The effect is congregational INVOLVEMENT in the Word. It's an excellent alternative to reading the psalm in unison.

Have your group try this. Pick a psalm, such as Psalm 150. Study the lines carefully. Decide how you can best express the words. Psalm 150 is a psalm of praise. You can shout certain lines. For another line, *you . . . can . . . say . . . each . . . word . . . slowly,* with strong emphasis on each word. You can sing another line. You can clap and stamp your feet, and shout "PRAISE THE LORD!"

An excellent resource: *CATCH THE NEW WIND* by Marilee Zdenek and Marge Champion (Word Books, Publisher, Waco, Texas, 1972). This is the best book I have seen for ideas in worship.

> If you're ready to have some new experiences in worship, we would like to provide a framework through which your own creativity may flow.
> —to be spontaneous
> —to be free
> —to be improvisational
> —to allow for moment-to-moment happenings
> —to make room for the movement of the Holy Spirit.
> You are encouraged to draw from the best of our "happenings."
> —pages 9–10
> *Catch the New Wind*

4. Song Writing

This is not as hard as you think. Divide the group into smaller groups of three–five each. Give them a melody, a familiar one. Have them make up words to the tune. Consider this activity in relation to specific topics or mini-courses.

Consider writing songs for fun. How about a song about your group? your church? your minister?

Have a jam session. Everybody bring whatever instrument they play. Maybe you could figure out an accompaniment for one of your original songs.

G. DRAMA

Drama need not be associated with full-scale productions. There are several ways to use drama which take little or no preparation. You'll want to know about these for your little "bag of tricks." If you have the time and the leadership for a one or two act play, you will be interested in the list of resources at the end of this section, pp. 91–92.

1. Role Plays

A role play is a short scene in which the actors are given a situation and act out the consequences of the situation. There are no lines to learn, no script. The procedure:

(a) Describe a situation, a problem, an issue which includes some conflict.

(b) Describe the characters involved, usually two–five people. Tell enough about the character, so the actor can imagine how he might react in the situation.

(c) Ask for volunteers on the stage area.

(d) Arrange them on the stage area.

(e) Describe the situation again, explaining how the scene begins.

Example: A son comes home and is about to tell his father that he's dropping out of school. The scene begins with the son walking through the door.

(f) The actors carry out the situation. Let the conflict build. Usually resolution won't occur, for the characters will be defending their own positions.

(g) Cut the scene before it drags. Let the scene progress long enough for the characters' points of view to be developed.

(h) Cut and discuss. Ask the actors how they felt about the characters. Ask the audience how they felt about the characters. Ask: How might a character have been played differently?

AN ALTERNATIVE

A very interesting technique is to cut the scene a little early. Wait for the players to "get into" the roles. When you see that they are really "living" the characters, call "cut" and have them switch roles. This means they are to assume the exact opposite position from that which they were just defending.

Have them carry on the scene in their new roles. Or, they could start the scene over.

ANOTHER USE OF ROLE PLAY

Sometimes you'll have a situation which could be played negatively one way and positively another. Have the actors play it twice—first, with certain actors being hostile; and second, with them being loving and reconciling.

For example: In the situation with the son coming home announcing he's dropping out of school, it could be played twice. First, have the father be angry and threatening. Play it again with the father trying to be understanding and reconciling.

When to use: whenever you are dealing with a topic for which a role play would be appropriate. It gives the youth an opportunity to get into someone else's shoes, to experience what it might be like to be a parent, a teacher, a poor person, a black, a bigot, a caring person, etc.

Note: The youth may be reluctant to participate at first; but, once they get started, they usually love trying out these situations. If they are slow getting started, try some easy situations.

There will be times when it won't work. If the group is extremely tired or overly silly, the role plays may not work at all. After trying a couple, you'll want to move on to something else. ALWAYS DISCUSS AT THE END OF EACH ROLE PLAY.

2. Tableaux

A tableau is a human still picture. It can be used effectively in worship services or in creative productions. Tableaux can convey a story related to a Bible passage or a current issue. For example, you could have one or two junior highs narrate a story. The remainder of the junior highs would act out the story in a series of still scenes. These scenes would be worked out ahead of time.

Lighting is the key factor in this kind of production. You need to secure a spotlight. The room is dark. The spotlight comes on the scene and holds for a certain length of time, depending on the script. In the dark intervals, the actors change positions.

3. Human Sculptures [13]

Human sculptures are similar to tableaux, except that there is no advanced preparation needed. Divide the junior highs into small groups of six–eight each. Tell them they are to make a human sculpture describing certain words. The following words may be used:

Love	Hate
Fear	Joy
Anger	Celebration
Alienation	Reconciliation
War	Peace

Announce the word. Give the groups four–five minutes to decide on their sculptures. Then call "freeze." Give the groups time to look at each other. You could "freeze" the groups one at a time, so everyone can see each sculpture. Call the next word . . . and continue.

When to use: anytime. It's an activity. It's movement. Use at retreats, church-ins, any event. It's good for group building too.

Note: You might make movies of the sculptures.

4. Machines [14]

Machines are similar to sculptures. Divide into small groups of six–eight each. Each group is to make a machine. One rule: It must have movable parts. In fact, every part (person) must move in some way. The machine can be authentic, such as an airplane, a cuckoo clock, or a pin ball machine. Or, it could be "just a machine"—with gears, levers, pumps, whatever.

5. *Skits*

Skits are for fun! Most junior highs have made up skits or tried some oldies but goodies. What you would probably like to know is where to find skits. So would I! I did run across one book with six skits and a lot of other creative ideas. It is called *Right-on Ideas for Youth Groups,* compiled by Wayne Rice and Mike Yaconelli (Zondervan Publishing House, Grand Rapids, Michigan, 1973).

You can also find 38 pages of skit ideas in *The Omnibus of Fun* by Helen and Larry Eisenberg (Association Press).

6. *Plays—Productions*

Junior highs enjoy putting on plays and musicals. If your group wants to, you'll have to do some evaluation and careful planning. First of all, the amount of time it will take will be a big factor. Of course, this will depend on the length of the play or musical. The longer it is, the more time will be required. Can *you* give a lot of extra time for rehearsals? If not, is there someone in your church who could give the time and be the director?

Are your junior highs willing to give their time to working on rehearsals, props, scenery, costumes? Talk it over with them. Perhaps you can find a short play which would take minimal rehearsals and simple scenery, props, and costumes.

Plays and musicals can be performed in the chancel or in a fellowship hall. Your production might be performed—

>during a worship service
>at a family night supper
>during the church school hour
>at a picnic
>at a retreat
>on a special night, just for the production.

Plan to do a lot of publicity.

Now, where do you find plays? One of the best sources is:

>The Contemporary Drama Service
>P.O. Box 457
>Downers Grove, Illinois 60515

The CDS has a wide variety of drama materials:

>—plays for chancel or fellowship room
>—productions—plays with slides
>—musicals
>—musical dance dramas
>—choral readings
>—folk rock liturgies
>—excellent Christmas and Easter presentations
>—coffee house materials
>—skits

You can obtain preview copies and a complete catalogue from CDS. Another source is KAIROS. They produce dialog dramas and one-act plays. Write to:

KAIROS
Box 24056
Minneapolis, Minnesota 55424

H. RESOURCE PERSONS

For any topic, you could probably think of some person who could bring information to your group. If you were considering a political issue, the governor or your senator might offer some insights. Or, if you were studying what wealth and fame can do to a person's values, invite a Rockefeller. Obviously, there are limitations. But, you should be conscious of the possibilities for every subject your group will consider during the year.

A most likely resource person is your minister. He could help your junior highs when they are dealing with questions of faith, beliefs, worship, Christian ethics, and the mission of the church. Church members who are serving as elders, deacons, teachers, or on task forces can be excellent resource persons.

While you are planning your year with the youth, try to find out the occupations and interests of your congregation. Surely you will be able to make some connections for your mini-courses and programs.

You'll also need to look at different agencies in your community for resource persons.

How to use resource persons: Except in the unusual circumstance, do NOT invite a resource person to lecture the group. Straight lectures rarely make it with junior highs. Have the guest sit in on a discussion. Direct questions to him. Create an atmosphere in which the junior highs will feel free to ask questions.

A technique which would put the resource person in the spotlight is the "interview forum," in which the guest is interviewed by you or by a youth. This takes place before the entire group. The group is free to ask questions.

I. DISCUSSION

I was not sure where to insert a few ideas on discussion in a section on methods, although I do have a few thoughts to offer on the matter. For as long as there have been youth groups, discussion has been the number one method (even though recreation might compete for first place.)

When the youth comes up to the leader on Sunday morning and says: "What are we going to do tonight?" the leader responds: "We are going to talk about . . ." And, that's the way it is Sunday after Sunday. We're going to *talk* about race, sex and dating, poverty, censorship, identity, drugs. Have you ever heard these evaluations of a fairly successful meeting?

"We had a good discussion."
"I got them to talk about it."
"At least they were discussing."

It doesn't seem to matter whether or not they really understood or got anything out of it, as long as they were talking.

It must sound like I'm "down" on discussion. I am, if that's the only method or activity a leader ever uses. If every week, the leader asks: "What do you think about . . ." and lets the opinions fly back and forth, there's something wrong. There is no purpose being accomplished. Granted, not every discussion should reach a resolution, but the discussion should have a context. You should be able to answer: Why are we having this discussion? It should fit into a larger plan. It is the poor use of discussion that concerns me.

There are so many good ways to use discussion. After all, discussion gives the individuals an opportunity to participate. Each person can share his own experiences, opinions, and feelings. It is a valuable method. That is why I am so concerned that leaders become aware of effective discussion techniques.

If you look back through this section, you will find that many of the exercises under "Group Builders" (p. 61) and "Values Clarification" (p. 70) use discussion techniques. The Group Builders had you discussing:

facts about yourself
your likes and dislikes
fears you had as a child
what you would take out in a fire
what you like about each other
ways to pray and celebrate.

Values Clarification had you discussing:

what's important to you
what you value
what you are proud of
a position you would defend.

The mini-courses in Section C contain many suggestions for using discussion appropriately. The following are just a few methods for involving your group in purposeful discussion.

1. Task-Oriented Small Groups

Divide the total group into smaller groups when you are dealing with a subject about which:

(a) you would like everyone to offer an opinion and share feelings with each other (something that cannot be done in a large group).

(b) you have several questions to answer. Each smaller group can work on a question. If the questions require research, have the necessary materials for each group.

(c) you would like a variety of responses to the same question or task. Example: When paraphrasing a Bible passage, each smaller group works out its own paraphrase.

Always have the task clearly defined for each group, either on newsprint or on slips of paper.

Have the groups come together and share their findings. It is wise to appoint a reporter in each group. You will find the small group method used in most of the mini-courses in Section C.

The best way to have Bible study is to use smaller groups.

2. Fishbowl

The fishbowl is a small discussion group within the larger total group. The small group (the fish) discuss while the larger group (the bowl) observes. An empty chair is placed in the smaller circle. If someone from the bowl wishes to comment, he occupies the seat, speaks, and returns to the bowl. The bowl remains silent throughout the exercise.

After the fish have finished their discussion (you would give them a time limit), you may open the discussion to the bowl. You can ask if there is anything the bowl would like to ask the fish.

This technique is used for:

(a) variety in discussion, to make it a little more interesting.

(b) reporting. When the junior highs have been working in smaller groups, the fishbowl offers a different way to report to the group. Each group would take a turn being the fish. You, as leader, should sit with each group of fish and interview the fish about their work.

(c) evaluation. At the end of a mini-course or series of activities, you could evaluate by using the fishbowl technique. Have a small group (the fish) discuss the evaluation questions.

Try using this technique with your planning group as the fish. Since they would have had a vested interest in a particular program, they should be the ones to evaluate, à la fishbowl.

3. Brainstorming

Brainstorming is a part of the problem-solving process. When you have a problem, you brainstorm all the possible alternatives for solving the problem. That is, you don't settle for one or two answers. Rather, you think up as many as you can, regardless of their feasibility.

Brainstorming can be used with almost any question. Look at the following questions:

Why do Christians pray?
How can the church serve the community?
What does resurrection mean?
What keeps you from being free?
Why do drugs appeal to youth?
What is special about Jesus?

There is no one answer to any of these questions. To brainstorm, you would ask the group to think about the question. Then, have them give as many possible answers as they can think of. List them all on newsprint. *Newsprint is a must for brainstorming.* There is one rule: Every answer suggested is listed. None can be debated. There is no discussion of any until the list is finished.

Then, discussion of each may follow. In some cases, priorities among the answers may be determined. For example: For the question on how the church can serve the community, the group may list eleven ways. After discussion, they may decide that three or four are the best ways.

Note: I repeat: It is very important that every answer be listed. This insures that every person in that group will have his contribution considered.

4. *Questions: How to Ask*

Not many discussions occur without questions. At least, it is usually a question that gets the discussion started. However, you may have experienced that deadly silence, when you ask a question and . . . *nothing.* So, you try to ask it another way . . . still nothing. You're bombing badly, and you don't know what you're doing wrong. It may be the way you're phrasing the question. The following are a few guidelines which may help.

(a) Stay away from the questions for which the answer is "yes" or "no." That makes for a short discussion, to say the least. Example: You ask, "Do you think Jesus should have healed on the Sabbath?" Three people say "yes." And, you're moving right along. Aha! You could have asked "why?" That's right. "Yes" and "no" questions are acceptable if you ask "why" or "why not."

(b) When you're thinking of questions to ask, the WHO, WHAT, WHEN, WHERE, WHY, and HOW are the best. Ask questions that require explanations.

(c) Don't let just one person answer. As in brainstorming, encourage more than one answer. Say something like:

"Anyone else have another idea?"
"Okay, what else?"
"Could someone add to that?"
"Anyone have a different idea?"

(d) Always acknowledge the answer. Don't be quick to tell a person he is wrong. On opinion and feeling answers, listen; show you are interested.

Act like the person has made a valuable contribution. Most likely, he has. Say something like: "Good point."

(e) A young person's answer can be very short. Encourage him to say more. Such as: "Hey, that's interesting. Could you explain it a little more?"

(f) Don't be afraid of silence. Give them time to think about answers. Pauses are deadly to you, the questioner. It's amazing how many awful things go through your mind in a mere ten seconds, like:

"Oh dear. They don't understand the question."
"I sure look foolish."
"Am I really that bad?"
"They must hate being here."
"Won't somebody please say something?"

The pauses don't seem long to the youth. So, have patience.

(g) Do rephrase questions. Sometimes this helps fill the deadly pause. And, it does help the youth to understand what you're asking.

J. RECREATION

Except for four or five "goodies" I keep in my little bag of tricks, I am not the one to be writing about recreation. So, I'll give you my favorite games and recommend a couple of books on recreation.

1. *A What?*[15]

There are several versions of this game. One is to start an object around circle to left saying, "This is a dog." Next person says, "A what?" Starter says, "A dog." Object is then passed to next person with same procedure, but "A what?" question is always relayed back to the starter, who in turn gives the answer, which is relayed back around the circle, gradually repeated a number of times.

Simultaneous with starting "dog" to left, he starts "cat" to right, with same procedure.

A popular version is to have a several-word description, like "A freshly baked peach pie" and "A jar of watermelon pickles," or "This is a shawl with a long fringe" and "This is a pair of galoshes, slightly worn but wearable." (The longer the line, the smaller the circle should be to enjoy it.)

In any version, fun comes when signals for "dog" and "cat" or others begin to cross each other halfway around circle, and players do not know which way to turn for "A what?"

Any object can be used, such as a salt shaker for the dog and a pepper shaker for the cat.

This is a great game to use when having junior highs and adults together.

2. Operant Conditioning

This game is based on the theory of positive reinforcement by B. F. Skinner, which you may remember studying in science or psychology classes.

The object of the game is to make a volunteer do a task without telling him a word about what he is supposed to do. Like a dog receiving pellets, when the volunteer makes a move in the right direction, he receives positive reinforcement from the group—in the form of clapping or pounding on the wall or table.

Begin by having a volunteer leave the room. The group decides what task he should do. For example: He should walk in the door, over to a coke bottle, pick it up, and hand it to a designated person. Or, the volunteer should go to a box, take out a book, and leave the room with it.

The tasks can be simple or complicated. You might have someone crawl under a table. Everyone in the group needs to know exactly what the volunteer is supposed to do so he can reinforce him correctly.

Call the volunteer in. He must figure out what he is supposed to do. If he walks in one direction, and there is no clapping, he knows he has to try another.

No speaking, moaning, or shaking heads. The only sound should be the clapping and pounding.

This game is funny, sometimes frustrating, but oh so exciting when the volunteer finally gets it. The whole room is shaking with the pounding.

You can use this game a lot, for every junior high wants to give it a try.

3. Zip Zap

Zip Zap is a circle game in which the participants must know who is seated to their left and to their right. The person on your left is your ZIP. The person on your right is your ZAP. The leader starts in the center of the circle. He point to a person and says: "ZIP, one, two, three, four, five." That person must shout out the name of the person to his left, his ZIP, within the count to five. If the leader points to a person and says: "ZAP, one, two, three, four, five," he must shout the name of the person to his right, his ZAP. If he fails, he takes the leader's place in the center of the circle. The leader takes his chair.

This is a good "getting acquainted" game, for it forces the participants to learn each other's names.

4. Name Charade [16]

Prepare a stack of stick-on name tags with names of characters, movie stars, celebrities, politicians, etc.

Stick one name on the back of one person in the group. Everyone looks at this name and pantomimes the character, until the person guesses the names. No talking or sounds of any kind. Strictly pantomime.

When the name is guessed, put a tag on another person's back.

Suggestions for names:

Little Red Riding Hood   Rip Van Winkle
Three Little Pigs   Scrooge
Elvis Presley   Mary Poppins
Tiny Tim   Donald Duck
Snoopy   The Harlem Globetrotters
Marilyn Monroe   Peter Pan
The Lone Ranger   Superman
Sonny and Cher   your local football team
Mickey Mouse   your youth group leader
The Pied Piper   your governor
Tarzan

5. *Ha Ha*

Participants lie on the floor in a jagged line with their heads on someone else's stomach. Have the first person lie down on his back. The second lies at a 90° angle with his head on the first person's stomach. The third lies at a 90° angle to the second, with his head on the second's stomach, and so on.

The first person says "Ha," the second says "Ha Ha," the third "Ha Ha Ha," and so forth, each person adding another "Ha." The ha's are to be said seriously, without laughing. However, it rarely can be completed without bursts of laughter. But, that's the fun of it.

RESOURCES

1. *The Omnibus of Fun* by Helen and Larry Eisenberg (Association Press, New York, 1956). It's an older book. It's huge—625 pages. It's fantastic!

2. *The Fun Encyclopedia* by E. O. Harbin (Abingdon-Cokesbury Press, New York, 1940). 1008 pages.

3. *Right-on Ideas for Youth Groups* by Wayne Rice and Mike Yaconelli (Zondervan Publishing House, Grand Rapids, Michigan, 1973). Lots of new ideas for crowd breakers, games, creative communication, scavenger hunts, simulation games, special events, publicity and promotion, skits, fund raisers, camping.

4. *Guide for Recreation Leaders* by Glenn Bannerman and Robert Fakkema (John Knox Press, Atlanta, 1975). Includes recreation ideas for all kinds of groups, including the physically handicapped. Games, dances, stunts, puppetry, songs.

Section C

Mini-Courses

Introduction

There are eleven mini-courses in this section. A mini-course is a "short course" on a particular subject. These are not study courses, in the academic sense. Rather, they are activities built around certain topics. The suggested length of each mini-course is four sessions. However, each could be carried out in five or six sessions. In fact, once you become familiar with the pattern of mini-courses, you can design your own by expanding any of the courses. The topics are broad in scope. I had to pick certain aspects of the subjects in order to create "mini" courses. Thus, there are many areas not covered in these courses.

Why four sessions? If your group meets once a week, four sessions on a topic seems to be a happy length. Any fewer and you risk losing the concentration of the subject area. Any more and you risk losing the concentration of the youth, if not the youth themselves. Of course, this does depend on your group. For example, if you have a youth club program with a consistent group of junior highs turning out every week, you could probably have a six session mini-course. Be flexible with these courses. Bring in resources and ideas of your own.

The important thing is that you examine your goals and the purpose for each course. Each mini-course has a section entitled "For You and Your Planning Group." It was suggested in chapter 4 that you enlist a planning group, composed of three or four junior highs, for each event, mini-course, project, whatever. The planning group is essential for the success of these mini-courses. You need these youth to help you plan and evaluate. Plus, it gives them an opportunity to participate in their program—not just in the activities, but in the decision-making. They become responsible for the mini-course. Their evaluation is important. You will see the mature side of junior highs when you involve them in evaluation of a particular course. And, you will learn a lot from them.

Sometimes it is hard to get the planning group together. Either you can't find the time or the youth are off in different directions. One of the best times might be after your group meeting. Call the planning group and ask them to stay 30–40 minutes after youth group. You will have to do some calling. Youth forget quite easily.

The "Preparation" section is a list of details you will need to do ahead for each session. As you read through the "preparation," you will find several items which should be dealt with by you and your planning group. Again, they can be a great help to you. And, you will get to know more of your junior highs individually.

You can give them responsibility in "gathering materials." But, do call to remind them and to make sure they are going to be there. If too many end up saying "I can't come tonight" after agreeing to do certain tasks, then it's time to call a halt and say something like: "Hey, look, the planning groups are falling apart. Those who have said they would do certain things are not doing them. I am ending up doing what you have agreed to do. What should we do about it?" The junior highs will have to come through with ideas to pull the program together. They do need to feel this kind of corporate responsibility.

A word about setting. Some of the exercises have specific instructions for room and seating arrangements. Where there are no instructions, you can assume the setting is a circle, with everyone seated on chairs or on floor. Sometimes, it is appropriate to be seated around a large table. The leader should sit with the group as much as possible. If the adult stands before a group of seated youth, the effect is strongly "I am the teacher; you are the pupil." Having the leader sit with the youth promotes comfortable adult-youth relationships.

Many of the mini-courses are more effective in groups whose members know each other quite well, who have worked at becoming a group. You will notice that several exercises would obviously work better with junior highs who are comfortable expressing their own feelings and opinions. I would suggest that you assess the group building needs of your youth. Spend some time on group building (see pp. 61–70) before you attempt a mini-course. The Value Process course incorporates several group building techniques. For this reason, you may want to use Value Process as one of your first mini-courses.

7

Value Process

Everyone makes decisions, small or large, every day. Everyone has opinions, ideas, and feelings about what happens in our world. Whether we realize it or not, all our decisions are based on our ideas, beliefs, and values. Value Process is a method by which one can discover what he values and why he values it. A more appropriate term for value process is values clarification. This method is best described in *Values Clarification: A Handbook of Practical Strategies for Teachers and Students* by Sidney B. Simon, Leland W. Howe, and Howard Kirschenbaum. This handbook contains strategies which can be used in a variety of ways: as a unit on values, as opinion-gathering exercises for study topics, for reflection and self-evaluation, for planning.

We live in a confusing world. It is hard to sort out all the input we receive. But somehow we make decisions and act according to . . . to what? How do we choose? By what criteria?

This course will give youth an opportunity to evaluate their feelings and opinions to find those which are most important, those which meet the following criteria of "valuing:" [1]

CHOOSING one's beliefs and behaviors
1. Did you choose it from alternatives?
2. Did you choose it after consideration of consequences?
3. Did you choose it freely (or were you greatly influenced by friends, family, etc.)?
PRIZING one's beliefs and behaviors
4. Do you prize or cherish your position?
5. Have you publicly affirmed it?
ACTING on one's beliefs
6. Have you acted or done anything about your beliefs?
7. Have you acted with repetition, pattern or consistency on this issue?

The basic objective is: that students participate in the exercises. Your aim is that they discover the values which direct their actions and that they act upon those beliefs which they consider important. You are not working toward consensus or group conclusions. There is no right answer. Some exercises cover so many issues that you may feel fragmented at the end of the session. Make sure the youth understand that the purpose of it all is to clarify (make clear) in their own minds what they think.

Part of the purpose is to get away from the wishy-washy "I dunno how I feel" kind of answer. Youth are asked to make choices. By the end of the mini-course, they should be seeking opportunities to act on their values.

SESSIONS IN BRIEF

  I. Session I
     1. Make Descriptive Name Tags
     2. A Question of Priority
     3. Strength of Feeling exercise
     4. Take a Stand
 II. Session II
     1. Voting
     2. Priority List
     3. My Average Day
III. Session III
     1. Interviews
     2. In My Opinion
     3. Pick an issue and develop a stand on it
     4. Fishbowl (on action problem)
IV. Session IV
     1. Fishbowl continued
     2. Brainstorm alternatives
     3. Self-contracts
     4. Telegrams

FOR YOU AND YOUR PLANNING GROUP

1. Read the entire mini-course carefully. Make sure you understand the purpose. Try out some of the exercises. Pick a value (something you consider important). Test it by the seven criteria.

2. Go over the exercises for which you'll need to make up questions in addition to the ones suggested.

3. If you have time and are interested, design your own valuing mini-course, using Simon, Howe, and Kirschenbaum's *Values Clarification.*

SESSION I

Purpose: To identify feelings, opinions, ideas on various issues.

PREPARATION

1. Read over session. Decide which Question of Priority questions to use. Make up others.

2. Make up list for Strength of Feeling.

3. Choose questions for Take a Stand. Make up others.

4. Prepare newsprint with A Question of Priority choices. Prepare newsprint with list of words for Strength of Feeling.

5. Gather materials
   —construction paper (at least 6″ × 8″) for each name tag
   —pins
   —felt pens
   —newsprint
   —large cards or sheets (8″ × 11″) with numbers for Strength of Feeling
   —paper and pencils, pens
   —blackboard

THE SESSION

1. *Descriptive Name Tags* [2]

As youth arrive, have them take a piece of colored construction paper. Each should write his first name on it (so it can be seen). Then, have them think of four or five words ending in "-ing" or "-able," which tell something about who they are, e.g., guitar-playing, tennising, trackable, happy-able. Obviously, the words do not have to make sense. Have them write these words anywhere on their large name tags, on the same side as their names. Then they pin on their name tags. Have everyone get up and roam around the room, reading each other's name tag, shaking hands, touching each other's nose or chin, asking questions, if they wish.

Note: The leader should participate too!

2. *A Question of Priority* [3]

This exercise gives each youth an opportunity to choose from among alternatives and to publicly affirm his position and explain or defend it if he wishes.

Explain to the group that you will ask them questions which will require that they consider options and make a value judgment. You will give them three or four alternatives for each question and ask them to rank these alternatives according to their own preferences.

There are several ways of carrying out this exercise:

(a) Have each and every youth give his first, second, and third rankings. Do not discuss.

(b) Have five or six youth give answers to the first question and explain "why?" they ranked in that order. Have the next five or six youth do the second question and so on. Brief discussion may follow.

(c) Use only a few questions. Use as starters for discussion.

Display the newsprint sheet with the choices. Read the questions.

The following are suggestions. DO MAKE UP YOUR OWN.

1. Which of the following would you like to do with a group of friends?
   ____go fishing
   ____go to the beach
   ____go shopping
   ____go hiking

2. Where would you rather live?
   ____the East
   ____the North
   ____the South
   ____the West

3. On which should our state be spending money?
   ____crime prevention
   ____education
   ____health services

4. If you had $300 given to you, would you
   ____give it away
   ____spend it
   ____put it in savings

5. How do you prefer to spend the summer?
   ____on a trip
   ____sun bathing
   ____goofing off
   ____working

6. You're going out to dinner. What's your choice of restaurant?
   ____steak
   ____hamburger
   ____Mexican
   ____Italian

7. Someone is getting robbed. Would you
   ____go after the robber
   ____scream
   ____walk on by
   ____find the police

8. A friend reveals to you that he is a pusher. Would you
   ____turn him in

————avoid him

————do nothing, but stay a friend

9. The clerk at a store gives you too much change, 90¢. You don't notice it until you get home. Would you

————keep it

————drive back and return it

————call the store

10. Someone leaves a shopping cart in a parking space. Do you

————push it back to the store

————do nothing

————ask the person to return it

11. Sex education should be taught

————in the church

————in the school

————in the home

12. I have strong feelings about

————women's lib

————abortion

————politicians

13. Do you wish you were great at

————a sport

————a musical instrument or singing

————getting good grades

14. If I had to choose from the following occupations, I would be:

————a prison guard

————a rodeo cowboy

————a taxidermist

15. The quality I would most like to have is:

————courage

————truthfulness

————popularity

16. If I could be any of these, I would like to be:

————president of the U. S.

————the richest person in the U. S.

————a movie star

17. If I had to choose, I would be

————very poor

————in prison

————sick

18. At a party, I'd like to be

————the funniest person

————the quietest

————the most sophisticated

3. *Strength of Feeling*

This is a fun exercise in which the youth will examine their own feelings, pro or con, positive or negative, towards the following value words:

School   1 2 3 4 5 6 7
Football
Politics
MASH (or some popular TV show)
Busing
Church
Women's Lib
Work   (Substitute words relating to relevant issues.)
College
Police
Peace

Pass out paper and pencils. Have them copy the list. For each word, ask them to choose the appropriate number which identifies their feelings and write it down after the word. A "1" indicates strongly NEGATIVE feelings. A "7" indicates strongly POSITIVE feelings. Caution them to stay away from "4", which is the "middle-of-the-road" number. If, however, there is a word for which they have no feeling one way or the other, then they would write a "4".

While the group is working on this, the leader takes the numbered sheets (or cards) and places them on the floor, about two or three feet apart, in a straight line.

| 1 | | 2 | | 3 | | 4 | | 5 | | 6 | | 7 |

After everyone has finished, show them where the numbers are. Explain that they are going to have an opportunity to "take a stand" on issues and see how they compare with others in the group. They are to take their sheets with them.

While they are moving toward the numbers, call out the first word. They should move to the appropriate number. They stand there only a few seconds, long enough to look around and see the distribution of the group.

Call the next word . . . and so forth.

Leader: participate!

4. *Take A Stand* [4]

Take a Stand is similar to the preceding exercise. The youth are to determine where they would place themselves between two polar positions on any given issue.

The leader suggests an issue and draws a long line on the blackboard.

The two polar positions (far left and far right) are established. He divides the line with marks:

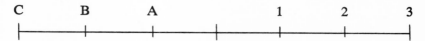

Each youth is to indicate where he stands on this issue. He may briefly describe his position, without giving reasons for holding that position. Later, he may share reasons, if you decide to discuss any of the issues.

Go around the room, asking each to state his position. Place the first name (or initial) on the line indicated by each person.

Caution against the middle. Encourage each to think for himself and not to follow the crowd. The following are suggestions. Think of your own.

1. How do you handle money?

2. How much TV do you watch?

3. How do you feel about the space program?

4. How much self-discipline do you have?

5. How well do you get along with your parents?

6. How competitive are you?

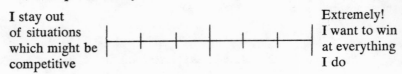

I stay out
of situations
which might be
competitive

Extremely!
I want to win
at everything
I do

7. How much time do you spend alone on an average Saturday?

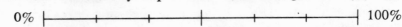

0%   100%

8. How important to you are your beliefs?

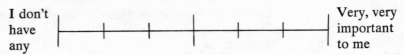

I don't
have
any

Very, very
important
to me

9. As you see yourself, how much common sense do you have?

No
common
sense
at all

I am
very sensible
about
everything

10. How politically active do you see yourself when you are 25?

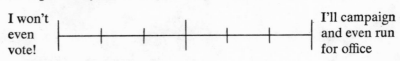

I won't
even
vote!

I'll campaign
and even run
for office

11. How do you feel about work?

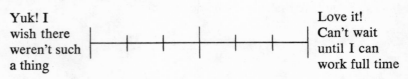

Yuk! I
wish there
weren't such
a thing

Love it!
Can't wait
until I can
work full time

12. How important is popularity to you?

Doesn't
mean a
thing

I want to be
the most
popular kid
in town

13. How much do your friends' ideas and actions influence you?

I do my own
thing with
no regard to
what friends
say or do

Everything I
do, I do
because
somebody else
does it that way

SESSION II

Purpose: To discover what I consider important by identifying what is important to me and how I spend my time.

PREPARATION

1. Read over the exercises carefully. Make up your own questions for the Voting (exercise 1).
2. Mimeograph the Value Priority list (exercise 2).
3. Gather materials
—mimeographed Value Priority list
—pencils, pens
—blackboard or newsprint

THE SESSION

1. *Voting* [5]

This is a good "starter" exercise. It requires that youth determine their positions on subjects. Voting occurs in such a way that no one stands out for voting differently from everyone else.

The leader reads a question. Each person raises his hand according to the strength of his feelings. If his answer is "yes" or "strongly in favor," he raises his hand high. If he is "against," he holds his arm down by his side. If "in the middle," he holds his arm straight out in front at a 90° angle to his body. Of course, he may choose a position in between low, middle, and high.

After the voting, proceed to the next question without discussion. If you are using this exercise to find issues for discussion, make note of those which could bring out strong feelings or divergent views.

The following are suggestions. MAKE UP YOUR OWN. All questions begin with: "How many of you . . ."

—would marry for money?
—like tomatoes?
—can change a tire?
—are in favor of mercy-killing?
—read a lot?

—can play bridge?
—are trying to conserve energy?
—would vote for a woman president?
—would vote for a woman senator?
—like TV commercials?
—like to go shopping?
—look for bargains?
—are afraid of thunderstorms?
—have ever been in a tornado?
—have ever been to an X-rated movie?
—would prefer to live at the beach than the mountains?
—would prefer mountains to the beach?
—would like to own a boat?
—have ever won anything?
—would marry a black person?
.—would marry a white person?
—would date a black?
—would invite a black home for dinner?
—would adopt a baby?
—do volunteer work?
—would hitchhike?
—would pick up a hitchhiker?
—have ever stolen something?
—want children?
—agree with your parents on political issues?
—agree with your parents on most everything?
—play a musical instrument?
—want to go to college?
—like yourself?
—like the way you look?
—have ever baked a cake?
—would visit a jail?
—would turn in a pusher?
—are patriotic?
—like to travel?
—like to come to youth group?
—believe in God?
—know what you believe?
—wish you knew what you believed?
—have ever babysat?
—have a lot of freedom?
—have ever signed a contract?
—would like to write a book?
—have ever been to the Capitol in Washington?
—would like to run for office some day?
—would bet money on a horse?
—would like to live on a farm?

2. *Value Priority List* [6]

The purpose of the list is to help the youth identify priorities in life. Pass out the Value Priority list (or display the terms on newsprint and have them copy the list). The participants are to arrange the values in order of their importance as guiding principles in their lives.

They are to study the list carefully and put a "1" next to the value which is most important, a "2" next to the second most important, and so on. The least important value will be ranked "18."

This will be a little difficult. You will wish you could put the same number next to a couple of values to show equal importance. Try to decide one over the other and use all 18 numbers.

The Value Priority list:

———— Honesty
———— Generosity
———— Achievement (accomplishments)
———— Faith
———— Happiness
———— Equality (fairness, justice for all)
———— Peace
———— Excitement (an exciting life)
———— Freedom (independence)
———— Health
———— Popularity
———— Courage
———— Open-mindedness
———— Wisdom
———— Practicality
———— Idealism
———— Self-control
———— Love

After all have finished, go around the circle, having each state his first three values. Next time around—his last two.

3. *My Average Day* [7]

Did you ever stop to think how you spend your time? What is your average day like? Do you waste a lot of time? The junior high spends a large chunk of his day in school—or in school-related activities.

But, what does he do with the rest of his day? This exercise encourages the participant to consider his day and how he might like to change the way his spends his time.

Have the youth copy the following list on the back of their Priority List sheets:

1. Sleeping
2. In school
3. Playing sports (or other extracurricular activities)
4. With family (meals included)
5. With friends
6. Doing homework
7. Alone
8. ——————————— (other)

Then have them estimate how many hours on an average school day they spend on each. They are to write the number after each. Remind them to make sure their numbers add up to 24.

Then they are to examine each item. Ask:
1. Are you satisfied with the amount of time you spend on each item?
2. Which would you like to change? Go ahead and make the changes. Write a revised number after each item.
3. Is there anything you would like to be doing which is not on the list? Add that and the amount of time you desire for it.

Have them look over the revisions. This is their "ideal" day.

Go around the circle, having each describe the changes he made.

Then, have them think of positive steps they can take to make such changes. There will be some over which they have no control. For instance, they might like to spend four hours in school instead of six, but that's beyond their control.

They should list these ideas on paper. They may or may not share their ideas, depending on time remaining.

SESSION III

Purpose: At this stage in a values mini-course, the youth will be given opportunities not only to voice opinions and feelings, but to develop their positions on various matters.

PREPARATION

1. Read over the session carefully. Make sure you understand the procedure for each exercise.

2. You will need to spend some time making up questions for the Interviews. The youth in your planning group can be of help here.

3. Gather materials
   —paper and pencils
   —newsprint—with list of issues (see exercise 2)
   —newsprint—with valuing criteria (see exercise 3)

4. About the room: You will need chairs which may be moved around for the different exercises.

THE SESSION

1. *Interviews* [8]

You have seen reporters interview politicians, celebrities, authors. They ask for opinions, feelings, positions. Now is the time for all good leaders to become reporters. In this exercise, the leader will interview two or three youth, one at a time. The young person has the opportunity to publicly take a stand and explain his position on various value issues.

Two chairs are placed in front of the group. The leader asks for a volunteer. He explains the ground rules:

1. You must answer every question honestly.
2. You may "pass" a question if you do not wish to answer.
3. No one is to speak except the person being interviewed and the leader.
4. At the end of the interview, the person interviewed may ask the leader any of the questions he was asked.

After the interview is finished, ask the group if they have any questions to ask the person being interviewed.

The following are suggestions for questions. MAKE UP YOUR OWN AHEAD OF TIME. Some of the questions introduce a topic. You may ask the volunteer further questions after he responds, such as: "Why do you feel that way?" "Did you come by your position by yourself?" "Who or what influenced your thinking?" In other words, elaborate on the topic where appropriate.

The interview should last five or six minutes.

Sample questions:

1. What do you think is the most serious domestic problem in our country?
2. What kind of aid should we give other countries?
3. What magazines do you read?
4. What's your favorite thing to do for relaxation?
5. What's the most significant book you have read recently?
6. What movie have you seen recently which was awful?
7. What do you like best about your school?
8. What do you like least about your school?
9. Do you believe in ESP?
10. What do you think about ghosts?
11. What was the happiest moment in your life?
12. What do you like best about your parents?
13. Where would you like to live in the future?
14. Where would you like to visit?
15. Do you want to get married?
16. Do you want to have children?
17. What do you think about women's liberation?
18. Why is your favorite teacher your favorite teacher?
19. Are you interested in environmental protection?
20. What do you think can be done to protect the environment?
21. What would you like to change about yourself?

22. Who do you think should be responsible for censoring books and movies?
23. What do you think about mothers working?
24. Would you like to live in another country?
25. Do you prefer grades (A,B,C, etc.) or Pass-Fail?
26. What kind of dress code should your school have?
27. What is your opinion on capital punishment?
28. What is your position on gun control?
29. What is your opinion on abortion?
30. Do you think there is too much violence on TV?
31. If you disagreed with a law, what would you do about it?
32. What opinions do you have on political campaigns?
33. How might we solve the race problem?
34. What makes you mad?
35. What is one thing you would like people to know about you?
36. Who is someone you admire?
37. What do you notice first about a person when you meet him?
38. What's the nicest gift you've ever received?
39. How important is your faith to you?
40. Do you believe in God? Why?
41. What would you change about your church school?
42. What is something you would like to learn how to do?
43. What is something you're afraid of?
44. What do you like to talk about with friends?
45. Do you think women should hold high government positions?
46. What is something you and your parents disagree about?
47. What ideas do you have for your future?
48. What would you say is your "issue"?
49. What would you like to do to help people?
50. What is something you feel strongly about?

The following is a list of value-related issues to be used for reference in the next two exercises.

Prayer in public schools	Women's Lib
Legal age for drinking	Violence on TV
55 mph speed limit	Natural childbirth
Old people	Mercy killing
Death	National health insurance
Population	Protests
Economy	Political campaigns
Ecology	Strikes
Energy crisis	Race relations
Environmental protection	Open housing

Hunting
Censorship
Marriage
Raising children
Mothers working
War
Foreign affairs
Poverty
Grades
College
Dress Code
Amnesty
Sex education
Premarital sex
Legalizing marijuana
Gun control
Busing
Prison reform
Crime prevention
Abortion
Income tax
Laws
Missionaries

Private/public schools
Interracial marriage
Church in politics
Church school
Church and youth
Infant baptism
Birth control
Other religions
Consumer protection
Welfare
Woman president
Our judicial system
Morality
Age for dating in cars
Volunteer army
West Point
Astrology
ESP
Exorcism
Space exploration
Funerals
Leisure

Change and add to this list. Produce the list on newsprint.

2. *In My Opinion* [9]

This exercise enables the youth to determine the strength of their feelings on issues. Display the list of issues, explaining that this list may help them think of different issues.

Ask the group to complete this statement:

1. I have very strong feelings about . . .

Allow a few seconds for thought. Then, go around the circle, having each complete the statement. They may elaborate and explain.

Do the same procedure for each of the following:

2. I have an opinion on . . .
3. I am not willing to take a stand publicly on . . . but I do have an opinion.
4. The hardest issue for me is . . .
5. I don't yet know where I stand on . . .

3. *Development of My Stand* [10]

In this exercise, each youth will work on developing his position on an issue toward which he has strong feelings. Pass out paper and pencils.

First, the youth are to pick an issue about which they feel strongly. Use the list on newsprint as a resource. Tell them they are going to test their position by the criteria of "valuing."

Display the newsprint sheet with the following criteria:

1. Did you consider the alternatives in choosing your position?
2. Have you considered the consequences (both good and bad) of the alternatives and of your position?
3. Do you feel it was your own choice, or were you highly influenced by other persons?
4. Are you happy with your position or belief? Proud of it?
5. Are you willing to affirm your position publicly? Have you?
6. Do you act on your position? Does your belief determine the way you act?
7. Do you act on your position repeatedly? Has it become a part of your pattern of life?

On their paper, the youth are to make a comment for each of the criteria.

Example: 1. Yes, I do.
           2. No, I haven't.
           3. Yes, I did, etc.

For each criterion they have failed to meet, have them think of things they can do, steps they can take, to make their position meet that particular criterion. They are to list these. Then, have them make a list of reasons for taking the stand they have chosen. "Why do you feel that way?"

4. Fishbowl

This exercise follows number 3 as a method of encouraging the individual in the position he took. The youth will have an opportunity to support him, to strengthen him on his stand.

Ask for a volunteer. Explain that he will sit in the center with four other volunteers (the fish group). He will explain his issue, his stand on it, and the reasons for his stand.

The four will ask him questions about his stand. They may ask the criteria questions. Where the individual is not sure what he should do about his stand, the fish group may suggest ideas. He may react to their suggestions.

The remainder of the group (the bowl) is spread around the "fish" in a circle. One empty chair is placed among the fish. If someone from the "bowl" has an idea, he may occupy the chair. Then he may speak. He returns to the bowl after he has said what he wishes. The "bowl" remains silent throughout the exercise.

You will probably have time for only one volunteer. Plan to start the fourth session with this exercise and other volunteers. Each volunteer should have about ten minutes.

SESSION IV

Purpose: By now the youth should be able to make some decisions about value-related issues. In this session, they will work on establishing behaviors consistent with their values.

PREPARATION

1. Read over the entire session.
2. Have the planning group try out exercise 2, "Taking Action."
3. Gather materials
   —plenty of paper and pencils
   —newsprint of the seven criteria for "Valuing."

THE SESSION

1. *Fishbowl*

Continue the Fishbowl exercise from Session III. Let two or three youth be in the fish group.

2. *Taking Action*

In this exercise, the junior highs will look at a variety of things, not just issues. They will be deciding what they can do to make desired changes in their lives.

Pass out blank sheets of paper. Have each person think of several things he would like to be able to do better or learn to do, or a goal he would like to set for himself. They are to write these down. Such items might relate to:

family	relationship with others
work	personality
sports	ways to use time
social	ways to use leisure time
health	

Have them choose the one which is most important to them. Write that down on the other side of the page, at the top.

For a few minutes, they are to think of actions they would need to take in order to accomplish their goal.

Now, the group members are going to help each other with their tasks or goals. Have someone start by explaining what he chose. Then, he should tell what actions he might take. Have the group suggest other actions to help him.

Explain that if someone has chosen something he would rather not share, he may pick another item. Continue until everyone has a chance to speak.

Note: If you have a large group, you should divide them into smaller groups of five or six each.

3. Self-Contracts

Based on this last exercise, suggest that each person write himself a contract concerning the actions he will take. This contract should contain a time limit. For example: One junior high might decide he wants to get along better with his parents. His contract might state that for one week, every time he gets into a disagreement with his parents, he will not yell at them. Instead, he will try to listen to their side. Another youth might want to read more. So, he contracts to read one hour a night for one week.

Have them work up the contracts, and, if they are serious about them, sign them.

4. Telegrams [11]

Have you ever wanted to send a telegram to the president, your senator, or some such person? Now is your chance. This may be just an exercise for the junior highs, and yet, it may encourage the youth to take some action at a later date.

The instructions are simple. Have the youth think back over all the issues they have been considering during this mini-course. Display the issues list for reference. Have them choose one about which they have a strong position.

They are to write a telegram, consisting of 15 words or less. The telegram should be addressed to a real person.

After everyone is finished, read the telegrams out loud.

5. As a culminating activity, ask the group to think back over the mini-course, and complete any one of the following open-ended statements:

    (a) I learned that . . .
    (b) I was surprised to find out that I . . .
    (c) It became clear to me that . . .

Go around the circle, having each complete a statement.

EVALUATION

1. Did you understand the purpose of this mini-course? If not, how might we have made it clearer?

2. Did any of the exercises help you in clarifying your own values? Which ones? In what way did they help?

3. How did you feel about participating in this kind of mini-course?

4. What might we have done differently?

8

Values: Theirs, Mine, and Ours

All our lives we are faced with the necessity of making decisions. As infants we sat in our playpens and chose which toy we would chew on. As our world expanded, we were faced with many more decisions, some simple, some complex. The formation of values begins at an early age. From his parents, a child has his first value training. He is greatly influenced by the way his parents think and act. Friends (peers) become the next group to influence him. Then, the church, school, society, television, and many others act as influences. Each group has its own set of values. Each attempts to convince the person that its way is the right way.

It isn't surprising that there is confusion of values. At an early age, a young person must constantly sort out the input he receives. Will he do what his parents say? What his friends say? What the law says? Will he believe what his school teaches? the church? How difficult it is for him to ever say: "This is what *I* believe. This is *my* decision."

This mini-course will enable the junior high to examine the value input he receives from the adult world (his parents), from society, and from the Christian faith.

SESSIONS IN BRIEF

  I. The first session consists of four value-related exercises which are designed to introduce the junior highs to values and valuing (the process by which one decides what is important to him). A discussion of television commercials in included.
 II. Adults meet with youth in this session and participate in value exercises, including the Value Priority List. A meal or snack is suggested, to be followed by role plays.
III. Session III will include discussion of the surveys filled out by the adults and a simulation game, "Life Is Just a Bowl of Pennies."

IV. The youth will examine how the Christian faith relates to the process of valuing and to the values held by youth, adults, and society.

Methods suggested: resource person
                    small group Bible study
                    value exercises

FOR YOU AND YOUR PLANNING GROUP

1. Read over the entire mini-course. Discuss the exercises and questions.

2. Plan to send out cards to the parents of all junior highs, inviting them to your second session. Since all parents may not be able to come, the group may want to invite other leaders or teachers who are not junior high parents.

3. Decide on the time schedule and the type of meeting for Session II. You may need more time than your usual length of meeting. You could start at 5:00 P.M., do parts 1, 2, and 3, break for supper at 6:00 P.M., resume at 6:30, and finish at 7:30. Or, you might want to have a 7:00 to 9:30 P.M. meeting, with a break for ice cream.

4. Plan to line up a resource person as soon as possible for Session IV.

SESSION I

Purpose: To examine our own values—what is important to me. What gives direction to my life?

PREPARATION

1. Go over the entire session. Think of value words in addition to those listed. Watch some television commercials. Make notes on the tactics used to get you to buy the product. What values are involved?

2. Prepare newsprint sheets—
   a. purpose (list all 4 session purposes)
   b. values list (part 2)
   c. values list (part 3)
   d. heading only—"What do parents worry about?"
   e. heading only—"Values in society"
   f. heading only—"Commercials appeal to . . ."

3. Gather materials
   —newsprint
   —felt pens
   —paper and pencils

4. About the room: Choose a seating arrangement—chairs in a circle, or the group might sit on the floor. Prepare a place to display newsprint—easel, or tape on wall.

THE SESSION

1. Display the newsprint sheet on the "purpose." Explain the purpose of this mini-course. Briefly tell them what is planned for the four sessions.

2. *Values—Mine*

(a) Pass out paper and pencils. Display the first list of values. Have the group copy the list.

_____ Honesty
_____ Generosity
_____ Love
_____ Achievement (accomplishments)
_____ Faith
_____ Happiness
_____ Equality (fairness, justice for all)
_____ Peace
_____ Excitement (an exciting life)
_____ Freedom (independence)
_____ Health
_____ Popularity
_____ Courage
_____ Open-mindedness
_____ Self-control
_____ Wisdom
_____ Practicality
_____ Idealism

Instructions to the group: Rank the values as to their importance in directing your life. Ask yourself: "What do I live by?" Which of these values are most important to you?

Put a "1" in front of the word that ranks as the top priority, a "2" next to the second, all the way down to "18."

Obviously, it won't be easy. You may be tempted to put more than one "1" in your list. You may have difficulty deciding which of two is the more important. However, try to put them all in order from "1" to "18."

Feel free to jot down a comment after some of the words explaining how you feel about them. For example, you might write:

"Courage is important to me, but I don't really live by it, so I didn't rank it as high as I'd like."
or
"Self-control is ranked pretty low, but I really think it is important. I'd like to have more self-control."

You do not have to write a comment after every word.

(b) After they have finished their rankings, divide them into small groups of four to six persons each. Have each person circle his top five choices. Look at them. Is that really you? How is it different from you? Go around the circle, having each share his first five choices and tell whether they describe who he is. If they do not, explain what is different.

(c) Have them pick out the one value that they would like to work on, to make it an important factor in their lives. Go around the circle, having each explain the value he chose.

3. Values—Theirs

Show the group the second list of values, the list which includes the kinds of values that might be important to adults and parents. Place this list next to the first values list. Have them look at both lists and choose the *three* which they feel are the most important values to parents. Go around the room, having each state his three choices. Put a single mark after each word every time it is mentioned. Tally the marks to find the top three.

The second values list:

_____ Loyalty (to a person or cause)
_____ Affluence (making a lot of money)
_____ Success
_____ Family security
_____ Moral integrity (high moral standards)
_____ Obedience
_____ Peace of mind
_____ Trust

4. On a clean sheet of newsprint, list the answers the group gives to this question: What do parents worry about? Use the brainstorm technique. Just list; do not discuss each item.

5. Values—Ours

By now, they should have become familiar enough with value words so that they can brainstorm answers to this question: By what values does our society operate? "Our society" refers to your city or town, to the United States, but not to the world.

Note: To give you an idea of society-related values, the following words are suggested. Think of more.

Greed	Loyalty
Power	Strength
Law and Order	Immorality
Stability (avoiding change)	Economy (get the best at the
Success (we're number one)	cheapest price)
Freedom	Achievements
Permissiveness	Competition
Democracy	Pleasure
Courage	Sex

6. Television commercials are good indicators of our society's values. They are designed to appeal to the consumer so that he will buy the product. Youth enjoy talking about commercials they like and ones they don't like.

Suggest that they think about commercials and answer this question: To what values do commercials try to appeal? List these values on newsprint. See if they can think of some slogans. For example:

Some appeal to pleasure.
"You only go 'round once in life, so you've got to grab for all the gusto you can get."
Some appeal to our need to trust in something.
"If you can't trust Prestone, who can you trust?"
"You can trust your car to the man who wears the star."
"You're in good hands with Allstate."
"Do you believe in peanut butter?"
Some appeal to wanting the best at the cheapest price.
"We've got the best deal in town."
"Better than the high priced spread."
"You get more for your money."
Some appeal to humor
kitty and dog food commercials

Suggest that they watch commercials this week with this question in mind: How is this commercial trying to get me to buy the product? What values are involved?

7. Tell them about next week's session. Describe what they will be doing with the adults. Encourage them to bring their parents. The junior highs may be reluctant to meet with parents unless you can assure them that the parents will not have any dominance in the meeting. Their opinions will not carry more weight than the youth's. Explain that they will be doing fun kinds of things. They will not have to worry about being "put down." Also, stress the point that even though an individual's parents cannot come, he should come anyway. After all, if two parents per youth did come, the adults would outnumber the youth.

Note: MAKE SURE YOU GET THE CARDS SENT OUT TO THE PARENTS.

SESSION II

Purpose: To examine adult/parent values. What is important to them? What gives direction to their lives?

PREPARATION

1. Read over and study the entire session.
2. Prepare a newsprint sheet with the list of words in part 3.

3. Have the Value Priority List mimeographed (part 5). (Value Priority List on p. 130.)

4. Study the role plays. Put them in the order of your preference. You may want to change the order once you get a feel of your group. Be flexible. Create other situations.

5. Arrange for the meal or snack.

6. Gather materials
—felt pens
—name tags
—newsprint sheets
—paper and pencils for everyone
—cardboard squares or sheets for part 3
—mimeographed Value Priority List

7. About the room: Scatter chairs around the room for the first activity. Note changes as the session proceeds.

THE SESSION

Make sure everyone gets a name tag, a piece of paper, and a pencil when he arrives.

1. *Ice Breaker*

Give the following instructions to the group: Look for someone you do not know very well. Youth should look for adults; adults look for youth. After everyone is paired, you are to interview them. Find out as much as you can about that person—where he was born, favorite food, hobby, favorite TV show, likes, dislikes—whatever you would like to ask him. Jot all this down on your paper. You both are to interview each other simultaneously.

After about seven minutes, call time. Arrange everyone in groups of eight to ten persons each. If you are in a home, use a different room for each group. Ask someone to start by introducing to his group the person he interviewed. Go around the circle until everyone has been introduced.

Note: The purpose of this exercise is to create a comfortable atmosphere for adults and youth, to make it easier for everyone to talk with and in front of each other. When the pairs are talking all at once in one large room, it will be chaotic. This confusion itself serves as an ice breaker.

2. In the same groups, ask each person to think of four items he would take out if his house were on fire (items other than people). List them in order of priority. Go around the circle, having each state the four items. This exercise tells you something about what you value.[1]

3. In this next exercise, the participants will examine their own feelings pro or con, positive or negative, towards the following value words:

Exams   1 2 3 4 5 6 7
Football
Busing
Income tax
Church
School   (Feel free to substitute words relating to relevant
Women's Lib   issues.)
Honesty
Work
Police
Peace
Politics

Pass out paper and pencils. Have them copy the list. For each word, ask them to choose the appropriate number which identifies their feelings and write it down after the word. A "1" indicates strongly NEGATIVE feelings. A "7" indicates strongly POSITIVE feelings. Caution them to try to stay away from "4" which is the middle-of-the-road number. If, however, there is a word for which they have no feeling one way or the other, then they would write a "4".

While the participants are working on this, the leader takes the numbered sheets (or cards) and places them on the floor, about two or three feet apart in a straight line.

| 1 | | 2 | | 3 | | 4 | | 5 | | 6 | | 7 |

After everyone has finished, show them where the numbers are. Explain that they are going to have an opportunity to "take a stand" on issues and see how they compare with others in the group. Have them take their sheets with them.

While they are moving toward the numbers, call out the first word. They should move to the appropriate number. They need stand there only a few seconds, long enough to look around and see the distribution of the group. Call the next word . . . and so on.

Adults and youth alike seem to enjoy this exercise. Moving back and forth keeps the group lively. It should not be a threatening experience. When someone finds himself the only one standing on a "1", it is only for a short time. He will experience for a few seconds what it is like to take an unpopular position.

Junior highs are willing to do this kind of activity with adults because everyone is entitled to his own opinion. What an individual believes or feels is not debated. No one is right; no one is wrong.
BREAK—for supper or ice cream.

4. *Role Plays*

The following are suggestions for role plays which can be used with youth and adults. Role plays give persons an opportunity to put themselves in certain positions (roles), whether they agree or disagree with the particular position. Following the situations are suggestions for discussion.

The most enjoyable part of adult-youth role plays is having youth take adult roles and parents take the roles of teenagers. Even though the dramatization is often amusing, some of the enactments can be very moving. Switching roles in the middle of the action is very effective, for then the participant has to assume the exact opposite position from that which he was defending. Discussion should always follow. The participants should have an opportunity to explain how they felt in their roles.

Instructions for the leader:

1. Describe the situation and the characters involved.

2. Ask for volunteers. Specify whether you want a kid playing the youth or an adult playing the youth. You may want to assign roles, especially if you don't have any volunteers.

3. Place the characters on the stage area and explain the situation again.

4. As to how long to let the scene progress, play it by ear. Watch the development of the characters. Give them time to "get into" their roles and the conflict.

You could: (a) allow the scene to carry through to some kind of conclusion or resolution of the conflict; or (b) at the height of the conflict, say "switch roles." Have the two opposing viewpoints switch. They may continue from where they left off. Or, they may start over.

5. If a particular scene is not working, you might switch roles to help get things going.

6. Watch the scene carefully so that you can ask specific questions about the characters. Some questions you will address to the participants; some to the audience.

Situations:

1. A young woman of 20, whose parents are bitter racists, has been dating a 22-year-old black man. She brings him home and introduces him to her parents for the first time and announces that she plans to marry him.

   Four characters—Father and Mother are bitter; Daughter is intelligent, mature, and in love; Black man is in favor of the marriage and in love.

   Using the same situation, have the daughter and black man leave the scene. Add a neighbor couple, close friends of the family. This man and wife are open-minded, caring, and can see both sides of the issue. They feel the daughter and boyfriend are not being understood by the parents.

The neighbor couple enter while daughter and black man are still in the room, on stage.

2. A 14-year-old girl has been asked out by a 17-year-old boy who has his own car. Her parents had previously allowed her to go to parties with boys as long as they or the boy's parents picked them up and did all the driving. Now the girl is asking for the first time to go out with a boy in his own car.

Three characters—Mother, Father, Daughter.

There are two scenes. In the first scene, she is asking permission from the parents. In the second scene, she leaves, and the father and mother discuss the problem.

Try using an adult for the youth, an adult for the mother, and a junior high for the father. Or, use two youth and one adult—youth as mother and daughter, adult as father.

3. A 17-year-old boy wants to hitchhike around the United States with another boy. The parents are very much against it. They like the other boy; that's not the problem. They are against hitchhiking. They are afraid of all kinds of bad things that might happen to him.

Three characters—Father, Mother, Son.

4. The grandmother of a 12-year-old girl is dying. The girl wants to go and see her grandmother whom she had last seen three weeks previously. The grandmother has changed drastically for the worse. The mother feels it would be harmful for the girl to see her grandmother in such a failing state. The father is undecided.

Begin the scene with the daughter asking: "Which day are we going to the hospital to see Grandma?"

Three characters—Mother, Father, Daughter.

5. A girl tells her parents that she is pregnant, that her boyfriend has left town, and that she intends to have and to keep the baby.

Three characters—Mother, Father, Daughter.

This scene should be played twice:
   a) First, with the parents shocked, angry, blaming; in a hostile atmosphere.
   b) Second, with the parents trying to work out the situation; in an atmosphere of love and understanding.

Suggestions for discussion:
   1. Ask the players how they felt in their roles. Ask how they felt when they switched to the opposing position.

2. Ask the audience for their reactions to the roles. Ask specifically, such as: How did you react to the father's argument? What did you think about the way the son acted?
3. Ask how the situation might have been handled differently.
4. Ask what values emerge. What are the prime motivations for the arguments? What is the basis for each person's position?

Make up your own situations. Ask the group to make up some.

5. *The Value Priority List* [2]

This survey of values is a combination of the two lists of value words used in the first session with the youth. Everyone is to fill it out, even those youth who ranked values the week before.

(a) Pass out the sheets. Have them put an A (adult) or Y (youth) respectively at the top of their sheets. They are not to put their names on the sheets.

(b) Instruct them to rank the values from "1" to "17" and answer the three questions at the bottom of the page.

(c) After they have finished, they should arrange themselves in the same small groups they were in earlier. Going around the circle, have each person state his first three choices. The second time around, have each state his last three, numbers "15," "16," and "17."

(d) For the three questions, take each, one at a time, and share answers around the circle.

(e) Collect the sheets.

To close the session, you could display the purpose sheet and describe what has been happening in this mini-course. Give them a preview of the next session.

AN ALTERNATIVE:

If the role plays are going well and you are running out of time, use the last 10–15 minutes for filling out the Value Priority List. Have everyone hand in the list. Do not discuss. You will then examine the lists with the youth in Session III.

VALUE PRIORITY LIST

_____ Happiness
_____ Open-mindedness
_____ Family security
_____ Success
_____ Courage
_____ Love
_____ Honesty
_____ Faith

_____ Self-control
_____ Moral Integrity
_____ Affluence (making a lot of money)
_____ Peace of mind
_____ Idealism
_____ Practicality
_____ Exciting life
_____ National security
_____ Justice for all

1. Briefly describe the most important qualities in a marriage.
2. What would be three criteria for raising children? What would you see as important in raising children?
3. If you could change anything in your life or about yourself, what would you change?

SESSION III

Purpose: To examine prevailing values in our society. What is important in our world? What gives direction to the society around us?

PREPARATION

There are two activities for this session:
  —a simulation game
  —a reaction to value priority lists with adults
1. Tabulate the results of the _Adult_ lists from last session. Add up the numbers given for each word.
Example:

4	Happiness	2	Happiness	5	Happiness	= 11
8	Success	4	Success	10	Success	= 22
3	Family security	1	Family security	1	Family security	= 5

Arrange the words in order from the least number to the greatest.
Example: Family security = 5   XX
         Happiness   = 11
         Success   = 22
The words with the lower numbers indicate greater value, that the adults rated them high in priority. Put an "X" after each word that received a "1". You should have as many "X's" as you did adults present. Using the same procedure, tabulate the _Youth_ lists. Prepare a couple of newsprint sheets with your findings.
2. Study Session III. Make sure you understand the simulation game.
3. Gather materials
   —300–500 pennies (as many as you can find)

—box or bowl for the pennies

—newsprint sheet of value words, which you used in Session I

—sheet on which you have tabulated the results of the surveys

THE SESSION

1. *Simulation Game*—Life Is Just a Bowl of Pennies

This game gives the participants an opportunity to choose various roles to play in a simulated society. It is a simple game in which the participants acquire (grab) an amount of pennies. They will have to make decisions as to what they are going to do with this money.

The game begins as the leader empties a bowl or box of 300–500 pennies in the middle of the floor and explains the following rules:

"When I count to three, with *one* hand you are to grab for as many pennies as you can. Then you may do what you want with your pennies. Let us assume this is your life's worth. you might:

—find someone to gamble with (pitch pennies).

—make a contract with someone, that you will pay them a certain amount of pennies if they will do "such and such."

—you can become a thief and try to rob others.

—you could hire someone to become a thief for you.

—you may organize in whatever way you'd like, such as establishing a bank or a welfare agency.

Be as creative as you can. You can even withdraw and not do anything. The only rule is: YOU CANNOT HURT ANYONE PHYSICALLY. Now, instruct the group to gather around the pile of pennies. Count: One, two, three, GO. Tell them to count their pennies, so they can compare with what they have left at the end of the game.

For 10–15 minutes allow them to carry on. See what develops. If some have gambled and lost everything, suggest that they figure out something else—either try to get some money back, or maybe help out someone else.

After about fifteen minutes, announce: THIS IS THE I.R.S. IT REQUIRES THAT YOU PAY EIGHT PENNIES TAX TO THE GOVERNMENT. Go around with the bowl and make sure you collect eight pennies from each player. If they do not have eight pennies, direct them to a certain corner of the room, called the JAIL. See what happens. See if any of the "wealthy ones" decide to help out a friend and pay what he cannot pay of his tax.

Or, perhaps someone will become bondsman and offer bail for those in jail. Bond might be a loan of the eight pennies. (If the game is dragging and there are several in jail, you may have to suggest the bondsman/loan officer idea.) See what develops over the next 10–15 minutes.

Call the game to a halt. Have everyone count their pennies and gather in a circle. One by one, have each person tell exactly what he did throughout the entire game. Ask how he felt at certain points. If there were generous people, ask them what made them do what they did.

Ask the following questions:

1. Did any of you find yourself doing something that wasn't really you or that you could not see yourself doing in real life?
2. Did any of you do something that shocked yourself? Did you find out something about yourself that you didn't expect?
3. How many feel they would do in real life what they did in this game? Why, or why not?
4. What values emerged in this game? (They may need to see the newsprint sheets on value words.)
5. In what ways is this game like our society? In what ways is it not?

2. *Results of the Priority Lists*

Display the newsprint sheets on which you've summarized the results of the Adult and Youth lists. Compare priorities.

Display the newsprint sheet from Session I, part 3, on which are listed parent-type values and the ratings given by the junior highs. Compare this sheet with the summary on the Adult list.

Ask the group: In what ways were you correct in your assumptions about adult values? Where are the differences?

Pass out the Adult lists among the youth. Have each read the answer on his sheet to the first question: "Describe the most important qualities in a marriage." Discuss. Do they agree? Disagree?

Use the same procedure for Questions 2 and 3.

3. *Open-Ended Statement*

Suggest that the group think about what they have learned in the past two sessions about adult values. Have them choose any one of the following open-ended statements and finish the sentence:

> I was surprised to find out that . . .
> I discovered that . . .
> I was pleased to find out that . . .
> I no longer believe that . . .

SESSION IV

Purpose: To examine Christian values and how they relate to my life, to my relationship to my parents, and to society.

PREPARATION

The purpose of this session is to identify Christian values and to compare them to the other values by which one might order his life. The group will examine barriers to directing one's life by Christ-like priorities. They will then decide what they might do to eliminate the barriers and to start living according to Christian priorities.

1. Read through the session. Look up the Scripture passages. Ask your minister or other resource person for other suggestions of Biblical references to values.

2. If you are having a resource person at the meeting, check with him and explain the session. Show him the list of value words you've been using. Ask him to help the group in identifying which could be considered Christian values.

3. Gather materials
   —newsprint sheets of value words
   —clean newsprint
   —felt pen
   —Bibles (RSV)
   —envelopes and paper
   —pens and pencils

THE SESSION

1. Begin by reviewing the three previous sessions. Suggest that the group recall the values they discovered were a) important to them, b) important to adults, c) evident in society.

2. Display the newsprint lists of values from the other sessions. Ask the group which of all the values could be considered Christian values. Which would the Christian faith advocate as values by which we should order our lives? Go down the lists, circling the ones the group chooses. If some are debatable, take a vote.

3. At this point, we need to look at some facts. What are "Christian" values? By what criteria would a Christian order his life? How do we know?

Have four people look up the following verses and write them on newsprint: Micah 6:8; Matthew 22:37–39; Galatians 5:22–23; Matthew 6:33. Display the verses. Ask the group to explain the meaning of each verse. What kind of values are described?

4. Ask the group to think about their own priorities in values and society's values. Then ask: If we were to take seriously our faith and respond to God by a reordering of our priorities, what values would be the top priorities? List their answers on a separate sheet of newsprint.

4. The next issue is: What keeps us from living by these values? Ask the group to be honest and start listing all those things which keep us from living with Jesus Christ as our top priority.
Example: —would not be popular
           —don't understand what it means

—too busy with school, sports, etc.

—never tried it

Use a clean sheet of newsprint and list all these barriers.

5. Now, what can we do to eliminate these barriers? What positive steps could we take to reorder our lives according to the values of the Christian faith? What changes would we need to make in the way we live? For each negative (barrier) listed, have the group brainstorm ways to eliminate it. What can we do? List their suggestions (positive steps) on newsprint.

Give the group a few minutes to look over the list of positive steps.

6. Pass out paper, envelopes, pens, and pencils. They are to write themselves a letter—"Dear Self." In this letter they are to write what they would be willing to do in the next few weeks: (a) to change their priorities of values. What would I do differently? (b) to better relationships with parents. What would I be willing to do? and (c) to relate to society differently—what I would like my life to be like after I am finished with schooling. By what values will I direct my life, my work, my marriage, my family, my relationships to people, to the church, etc.?

Have each address the envelope to himself, insert the letter, and seal the envelope.

Collect the envelopes. Tell them you will mail the letters in six weeks. (Don't forget to mail these letters!)

EVALUATION

1. Look at the purposes for the four sessions. Do you think they were accomplished? In what ways?

2. What was the most meaningful part of this mini-course?

3. What questions do you still have about values?

4. What might we have done differently?

9

Identity: Who, Me?

A course on Identity for junior highs could take a whole year. This age group is in the process of establishing their personhood in a very confusing world. Their parents treat them like children and at the same time expect them to act like adults. Friends exert a great influence— both positive and negative. Appearance, personality, and popularity are so important. Unfortunately, the self-image is a little shaky. If a junior high does not see himself as attractive, popular, or liked, he can be shattered.

The church can play a positive role in affirming the junior high. In this mini-course, the leader needs to create an atmosphere of acceptance. The youth must feel that he is free to express himself without criticism.

Four areas of identity are explored here:

> strengths
> peer group influence
> worries and disappointments
> conflict

SESSIONS IN BRIEF

I.   First, strengths—not strengths and weaknesses—just *strengths*. We're hoping to get this course off to a positive start—having the youth feel good about themselves.

II. Your *peer group* is very influential in the development of your identity. In the second session, the youth will consider: How important are my friends in determining my behavior?

III. In Session III, the youth will have an opportunity to explore *worries and disappointments*. What does a junior high worry about? He has plenty of disappointments. Hopefully, he will feel comfortable enough in the group to talk about his disappointments. Part of group building is building a caring community.

IV. What part does *conflict* play in a junior high's life—conflict with parents, with family, with friends, with teachers? In this session, junior highs will discover creative ways to deal with conflict.

SESSION I

Purpose: To discover my strengths.

PREPARATION

1. Read over the session carefully. Consider the question: What could people do to bring out the strengths in me? Discuss with your planning group.
2. Gather materials
   —paper, crayons, pencils

THE SESSION

1. *A Picture of Me* [1]

Give each person two sheets of paper, pencil, and crayons.

The instructions for the first sheet are: Think of four major interests that make up your world and draw a symbol for each. For example, if athletics is a major interest, draw a football or tennis racquet. If making money is of major importance, you might draw a dollar bill.

Then, color each symbol in a color that expresses your feelings about that area of your life. Maybe you're not making much money, so you color the dollar bill gray.

Now, ask each person to choose a color that represents his outlook on life at present. Fill in the background around the symbols with this color. (Leader: participate in all the exercises in this session.) After everyone has finished, go around the circle, having each person explain his symbols and colors.

Ask the group: Did anyone learn something about another person, something he didn't know before?

2. *Strengths—Weaknesses*

Taking the second sheet of paper, the youth are to list on one side all their strengths—their good points or qualities. Give them about five minutes for this. Encourage them to be honest.

After they have finished, have them turn the sheet over and list weaknesses or bad things about themselves. Again, give them five minutes.

After all have finished, ask: Which list is longer? The "weakness" list usually is. If this is true of the majority, ask them why they think this is so. Why is it easier to think of bad qualities about ourselves? List their answers on newsprint.

3. People Can Help

Tell the group that in this exercise they are going to figure out what people can do to bring out the strengths in us. First, have them look over their "weakness" list and check those which they believe could become strengths with help from other people. For example, if one of my weaknesses was "giving up too easily," I might say that if people would encourage me more, I 'wouldn't give up so easily.

Go around the circle, having each person choose one weakness and tell how other people might help him.

Have them look over their "strength" list. Ask: What can people do to bring out a certain strength in you? For example, one of my strengths might be "caring for people." I would say that people can really help me by letting me know when someone is hurt or unhappy, because I would like to show that I care.

Using the same procedure, have each person choose one strength and explain how other people can help.

Tell everyone to listen carefully, so that they might know how to help others.

4. Strength Bombardment [2]

This is an exercise which will really make you feel good. Arrange the chairs in a horseshoe with an empty chair at the open end. One at a time, each person will sit quietly in the chair and be bombarded with affirmations. You may go around the circle in turn. Or, just have people speak out at random. Everyone is to say something he likes about the person or about a strength he sees in him. All comments are to be AFFIRMATIONS; no negative comments.

Tell the group to really build up the person. Encourage him. Each person should have a turn at being affirmed.

Note: If you have ten or more youth, you will probably want to break into two or more groups for exercises 3 and 4.

SESSION II

Purpose: To determine the kind of influence my peer group has.
           To express individuality.

PREPARATION

1. Go over the session carefully. The planning group can be helpful in identifying characteristics about their own peer group. Discuss the entire session.

2. Gather materials
   —newsprint
   —felt pens

THE SESSION

1. *Time Capsule*

Explain to the group what a time capsule is. It is a container which can be sealed and saved for future generations. It contains various items and information characteristic of the time in which it was prepared. Time capsules are usually placed inside cornerstones of new buildings.

In this exercise, the youth are to decide what items and facts should be put in a time capsule to tell the world a hundred years later what junior highs in 19__ were like.

Have someone list the items and facts on newsprint. If you wish, it would be fun to split the group in half, letting each group do the same task.

They should have 10–15 minutes to work on their lists.

2. *Comformity—Noncomformity*

On a newsprint or blackboard, make two columns, and head as follows:

Everybody does it	I wouldn't be caught dead . . .

Have the junior highs think of:

(a) things they do because everybody does it. It could be things relating to clothes, ways of acting, talking, places to go, things to do, things to like.

(b) things they wouldn't be caught dead doing, things that would embarrass them or cause them possible rejection from friends.

Now, have them think of things that they would be willing to do, even though it would be unpopular. In other words, what do you do that's just "you," something that points to your individuality?

Since this part of the exercise emphasizes individuality, each person should have a different answer. Go around the circle.

3. *The Real Me*

The instructions are: Find an object, any object, in this room (or house), which will symbolically represent who you are—"the real me." Find the object. Study it. And, bring it back to the circle.

For example: Someone picks up a yellow book. He explains: "This is the real me. I am hard shelled on the outside, like this hard cover. The yellow shows that I get along with people and laugh, even though something may hurt me. But, inside, you see pages and pages of fine print, showing that I am very complex and full of thoughts. The print is black, which shows that I am not always as happy as I appear on the outside."

When everyone has returned to the circle, have each person explain his object, "the real me."

SESSION III

Purpose: To explore worries and disappointments and to find ways to deal with them.

PREPARATION

1. Read over the session carefully.
2. Mimeograph the letters (part 3). Or, you could put them on newsprint. Make sure everyone will be able to see them.
3. Gather materials
   —letters (mimeographed or on newsprint)
   —newsprint (one sheet headed: "Things that make me mad")
   —felt pens
   —paper and envelopes
   —pens, pencils

THE SESSION

1. *Things That Make Me Mad*

As the kids arrive, direct them to a large newsprint sheet (on the wall or floor), which is headed: "Things that make me mad." Suggest that they all add to the list.

2. *Dear Me*

Pass out sheets of paper and envelopes. Have everyone write a letter to himself, telling all the things he's worried about right now, all the things that bothered him this week.

Have them address the envelopes to themselves, insert letter, and seal it. Collect the envelopes. Tell them you'll mail them in six weeks. It will be interesting to see how many of the "worries" have disappeared by then.

3. *Dear Helpful Hannah*

Dear Hannah,
   My grades this past nine weeks have not been good, but not real bad. My parents have been getting on me. They ground me when I get bad grades. They expect me to get A's in everything. I try real hard, but it's just not working. And, when I'm grounded, I get so angry inside I just can't study.

What can I do?

Allan Anger

Dear Hannah,

Boy, have I got a problem, or at least, it seems like that to me. I have a little sister that follows me every place I go, and if I tell her not to, she tells my mom, and I get into trouble for not being fair to her. When I'm outside talking with my friends, she comes out there and just sits and listens to everything we say. If I tell her to leave us alone, she goes and tells my mom. Then, my mom comes outside and calls me in. It embarrasses me in front of my friends.

I've tried to reason with my mom, but she never will let me express how I feel. She always tells me what I do wrong.

Please, give me your advice!

Girl with lots of problems

Dear Hannah,

I am so tired of being told what to do! I wish I could talk to my parents. But, it's no use. All they have to say is what I should be doing or what I shouldn't be doing. It's really getting me down.

Picked on

Dear Hannah,

I have a friend who is nice, but she sometimes acts mean to me. I don't know how to talk to her, because she gets mad real easy. I'd like to be honest with her, but I don't want to get her mad at me. What should I do?

True friend

Either mimeograph or copy these letters, one on each newsprint. Choose one which the group will use in writing an answer letter.

(a) Display the letter chosen. Give everyone time to read it (or read it to them). Divide into small groups of five or six persons each. Each group is to play the part of Helpful Hannah. They are to decide what kind of an answer they would give to this junior high's problem and work on a letter giving advice. Let them work for 10–15 minutes.

Bring the groups together. Have one person from each group read their letter. Discuss the differences.

Alternative: Have small groups work on different letters, instead of all groups working on the same letter.

Then ask: How would you evaluate the letters you wrote in light of the Christian faith? What advice would you consider Christian? Is there a difference in the kind of advice you'd give? Why? Discuss.

(b) Display another letter. Ask the total group what advice they'd give to this person. Do the same procedure with other letters, if you have time.

SESSION IV

Purpose: To discover creative ways to deal with conflict.

To develop a model for dealing with conflict.

PREPARATION

1. Go over the session.
2. Gather materials
   —clay
   —newspaper (to protect tables when using clay)
   —newsprint
   —felt pens

THE SESSION

1. *Clay Sculpture*

Give each person a lump of clay. Each is to make a sculpture representing "conflict." Give the group 15 minutes to work.

After all have finished, gather in a circle and let each person explain his sculpture.

2. *Conflict*

(a) Ask the group to think of situations in which they experience conflict. List on newsprint.

(b) Tell the group: "We are going to try to work out a theory or model for dealing with conflict. This model should work (or at least be tried) when we are in the midst of a conflict."

IDEAS first—What could you do when you get into a conflict? What are some possible outcomes? I win. You win. No one wins—compromise. Take one of the situations you have listed on the newsprint. Describe an example of that situation. Go into detail. Dramatize it. "So and so said, and then, I said. . . ." The object here is to visualize a concrete situation of conflict.

Then ask:

How does it usually end?

How would you like to see it end? (Write on newsprint the end desired.)

How could the conversation and actions proceed in order to achieve the desired end? (Describe in detail.)

Now, look at the conflict situation in its new setting.

What is the clue toward resolution?

What made resolution of the conflict possible?

Can we make up a theory incorporating the solution for conflict discovered in this situation?

Complete this statement:

The best way to deal with conflict is . . .

EVALUATION

1. What did you think was the most important thing about this mini-course?

2. Which session did you like the best? the least? Which activities did you like the best? the least?

3. Finish any one of the following sentence stems:

I learned that . . .

One thing I found out about myself was . . .

I'd like to change the way I . . .

4. Would you like to spend more time on one of the four topics? Which one?

5. What do you think we should have done differently?

10

Relationships

Life is made up of relationships. At every age we are learning how to relate to friends, to family, to God, and to our society. In fact, we are constantly learning how to relate to ourselves. You may have heard people say: "You can't love someone else unless you love yourself." There is a lot of truth in that. It is important to be able to accept yourself. But it isn't always easy. Take a sheet of paper. On one side list all of your strengths, your positive qualities. Then, turn the sheet over and list your weaknesses, what's wrong with you. Which list is longer? For some reason, the negative list usually wins.

Books have been written on "how to" get along with yourself and "how to" like yourself. Many "how to's" tell us how to get along with people; one of the developmental tasks of the junior high age is "accepting oneself." It is an awkward age physically. And emotionally, junior highs vary from day to day—ups and downs. Making mistakes is a tragedy for them. They do and say the wrong thing frequently. What is sad is that they cannot shake off the "wrongs" very easily.

Junior highs need acceptance—as we all do—both from friends and from adults. The Good News of Jesus Christ should be "good news" for these kids, for the Good News is—YOU ARE LOVED. YOU ARE ACCEPTED. It is our responsibility as the church to create an atmosphere of acceptance. They need to *feel* it, to feel wanted and acceptable.

SESSIONS IN BRIEF

This mini-course deals with relationships in terms of acceptance, love, and understanding.

I. First, the junior highs will look at themselves—"Who am I?" "I like me!" "Me and I get along." The goal is that they accept themselves, even though they can list eighty things they don't like about themselves.

II. The purpose of Session II is to discover the love of God and how it affects them personally.

III. In Session III, they will consider relationships to people by asking: "Based on my relationship to God, how do I relate to my neighbor?"

IV. Session IV asks: "Who is my neighbor?" The youth will brainstorm ways to relate to the large group of neighbors—the world.

FOR YOU AND YOUR PLANNING GROUP

There is not too much to prepare for this mini-course. Make sure that you study the entire course carefully and that you understand the purpose and the exercises.

SESSION I

Purpose: To begin to discover "Me."
To affirm each person in the group.

PREPARATION

Gather materials for collage
—large posterboard, usually 22″ × 28″ and available in a variety of colors
—magazines and newspapers
—glue
—scissors
—felt pens

THE SESSION

1. *Collage—of "Me"*

As the junior highs arrive, direct them to the materials. Tell them that they are going to make a "Me collage," a creative representation of who they are. They can look through magazines for pictures, words, or phrases. The collage can include interests, talents, moods, likes, dislikes.

"This collage will tell us all about you. It will help us to get to know you better." They have 20–30 minutes to make the collage, so they should get started right away.

After everyone is finished (or time has run out), have everyone bring his collage and sit in a circle, preferably on the floor (especially if you have a rug). Each person is to explain his collage.

2. *Adjectives to Describe "Me"* [1]

Everyone remains in the circle.

(a) Ask each person to think of two adjectives *he* would use to describe himself. Then go around the circle, each giving his two adjectives.

(b) Now, ask each to think of two adjectives his *parents* would use to describe him. Again, go around the circle.

(c) Then, ask each to think of two more adjectives, this time two which his *friends* would use. Go around the circle again.

3. *Silly Fears*

Ask each to think of a silly fear he had as a child about growing up. For example:

> "I was afraid of having to kill spiders by myself someday. My mother or dad always killed them for me."
>
> "I dreaded the thought of going into the army, because I'd have to eat their food. I'd heard it was the worst thing on earth. I wasn't worried about fighting, just the food."
>
> "I dreaded the day when I'd have to plug appliances into a socket."

Go around the circle, each explaining his silly fear.

4. *Strengths and Weaknesses*

Have them complete this statement: AS I SEE MYSELF, MY GREATEST STRENGTH IS . . .
Go around the circle. Then, have them complete the following: THERE'S A COUPLE OF THINGS I DON'T LIKE ABOUT MYSELF, LIKE . . .
Go around the circle again.

5. *Strength Bombardment* [2]

This exercise gives each person a chance to receive praise, encouragement, and good feelings from the members of the group.

Arrange the chairs in the shape of a horseshoe. Place an empty chair at the open end. One at a time, each person in the group will sit quietly in the chair and be bombarded with affirmations. Go around the circle, having each person say something he likes about the person. For example, "I really like your sense of humor," or "You say what you think. I admire that." AFFIRMATIONS ONLY, not negative comments.

Each person should have a turn at being affirmed.

SESSION II

Purpose: To identify my relationship to God. What is God like? How can I relate to him?

PREPARATION

1. Read over the session carefully.

2. Discuss within your planning group your own best experiences of worship and times you have felt a relationship to God (see exercise 3).

3. Share ideas on what you think it means to be created in the image of God (exercise 1).

4. Mimeograph the story "Goin' Home" (exercise 2).

5. Find a recording of "Tie a Yellow Ribbon Round the Ole Oak Tree," by Irwin Levine and L. Russell Brown. It was recorded by the group Tony Orlando and Dawn.

6. Gather materials
—mimeographed sheets
—recording of "Tie a Yellow Ribbon . . ."
—newsprint
—felt pens
—art materials, such as clay, paper, crayons (see exercise 4).
—Bibles (*Good News for Modern Man*)

THE SESSION

1. *Ideas*

You are interested in hearing each other's ideas in response to this question:

What does it mean to be created in the image of God?

Jot down ideas on newsprint. Encourage more than one or two answers.

2. *Goin' Home—The Prodigal Son*

The following is a story taken from J. Wallace Hamilton's *Horns and Halos in Human Nature*.[3] It should be mimeographed and distributed to the group.

Goin' Home

A friend of mine, the late G. W. Rosenbery, told me a story out of his early ministry. He was in a railway coach speeding across the state to attend a conference. Few people rode on trains in those days, and one boy in his late teens, apparently very nervous, attracted the attention of his fellow passengers. The boy was fidgety and restless. He would sit in one seat for a few moments, then move down the car to another.

The minister began to watch him and study him; finally he sat down beside the boy and said, "What's troubling you, son? Worried about something? Maybe I can help you. I am a minister, and if you feel like telling me, I should like nothing better than to help you if I can." "Sure, sure," the boy said, "I don't mind telling you. Are you acquainted in a little town named Springvale?" "Well, not exactly. I know of it. It is the next stop, isn't it?" "Yes," said the boy. "We'll be there in fifteen minutes. That's my home. I used to live there. My father and mother live there still, just a mile on this side of the town. Three years ago I had a quarrel with my father. I said, 'You'll never see me again.' I ran away from home. Three years, and they've been tough years. Sometimes I wrote to my mother. I wrote her last week and told her I would be on this train passing through. I told her if it was all right for me to stop, to hang something white outside the house so that I would know that father had agreed to let me stop. I told her not to do it unless father wanted it. She would do it regardless, you know, but I had to know how Dad feels."

The boy looked out the window, then started up excitedly. "Look, sir, my house is just around the bend, beyond the hill. Will you please look for me, see if there is something white? I can't stand to look. If there isn't anything white—you look, please!" The train lurched a bit as it made the slow curve, and the minister kept his eyes on the round of the hill. Then forgetting his dignity, he fairly shouted, "Look, son, look!" There stood a little farmhouse under the trees, but you could hardly see the house for white. It seems that father and mother had taken every bed sheet, bedspread, tablecloth, pillowcase, and even handkerchiefs, and hung them out on the clothes line and the trees. The boy's face went white, his lips quivered. He couldn't talk. His nervous fingers clutched the cheap suitcase, and he was out of the car before it had wholly stopped at the water tank. The minister said that the last he saw of him, he was running as fast as his legs could carry him, up the hill to the little house where the white sheets fluttered in the wind.

Give the group time to read the story. Ask if it sounds familiar to anyone? Hopefully, someone will mention the Prodigal Son story. (Don't be surprised if they don't.) They may think of the song: "Tie a Yellow Ribbon Round the Ole Oak Tree."

Pass out Bibles and have everyone look up Luke 15:11–24 and read silently. Divide the group in half. Have one group work on the story "Goin' Home," and the other on the passage of the Prodigal Son.

The task of both groups is:

1. Briefly state the facts of the story. What happened?
2. Write a biographical sketch of the son. What was he like?
3. Write a biographical sketch of the father. What was he like?
4. What might this story tell us about God? List some things.

Note: If you are limited by time, answer only Question 4. Come together and compare stories.

Ask Question 1.

Have Group 1 report.

Then, Group 2.

Ask Question 2.

Group 1 answer.

Then, Group 2.

Continue in the same manner with Question 3 and 4. On Question 4, were the two lists similar? Where did they differ?

Play the song: "Tie a Yellow Ribbon Round the Ole Oak Tree." Any similarities to the two stories?

3. *Open-ended Statements*

With everyone in a circle, have each finish this sentence:

I feel a relationship to God when . . .

Go around the circle for responses. Then, do the same procedure for:
My best experience of worship was . . .

4. *Creative Response*

Divide into three smaller groups. Have each group work on a creative presentation in answer to this question:

How would you describe God to a person who could not hear?
The presentation may be dramatic or artistic. Have clay and paper available for those who desire it.

Explain that this will be challenging, for you will not be able to speak, explain, or make any kinds of sounds. Allow them as much time as you can. Have each group give its presentation.

Note: There is no rule that everyone has to be in the final presentation. For example, if the medium were interpretive dance, the group could direct one or two of its members in the dance. And, all would participate in the direction.

SESSION III

Purpose: The question for this session is: "Based on my relationship to God, how do I relate to my neighbor?" Using a problem solving technique, the youth will discover ways to do just that.

PREPARATION

The only preparation required is the understanding of the procedures in this session. The only materials are plenty of newsprint and felt pens.

THE SESSION

1. *Ideas*

Draw on the board or newsprint the following columns:

Positive	Negative

Have the group think of how they relate to friends, and list some of the positive ways and the negative ways.
Example: avoiding someone they don't like—Negative.
laughing when someone says something funny—Positive.
teasing—Positive? Negative?
lying—Negative.

Give them plenty of time and encourage them to think of as many as they can.

2. Looking at the chart, discuss "which ways of relating to people I like." They may admit liking some of the negative ways.

Then, ask: Which items are ways which are *not* based on a relationship to God? In other words, which could be considered non-Christian? Why?

3. Then, consider how we can change the negative non-Christian ways of relating to people into positive ways, based on our relationship to God. Discuss those which could be changed. Ask: Would you be willing to change in that way? Why, or why not?

4. Problem Solving

Suggest that they think of some problems (actual problems, not made-up), that they have in relating to people. List these.

Have them choose one problem. Write it at the top of a clean newsprint sheet. Ask if everyone *understands* the problem, because you're going to try to solve it.

Then, think of the *desired outcome*. If the problem is a negative way of relating to people, then the desired outcome is some positive way. Define it. Write it down.

Now, ask the group to *brainstorm ways* to achieve the desired outcome. They should come up with lots of suggestions, even if they seem unrealistic or silly. Write them down.

Then, ask them to *choose* from the alternatives the ones they think are the best, the ones they'd be willing to try. Put a check by those.

One more task: Take each chosen alternative and discuss the problems you may encounter trying to carry it out.

Conclude. What did you decide? Do the chosen alternatives require a change in your behavior? Can you do it? Are you willing to?

Do another problem, if you have time.

SESSION IV

Purpose: Relationships are carried one step further as the youth explore "Who is my neighbor?" Who do we relate to in our society? And how are we to relate to them?

PREPARATION

1. Read over session. With the planning group, consider the questions about people in society and how we relate to them. What ideas does your planning group have?

2. Gather materials
     —a few newspapers

—newsprint
—felt pen

THE SESSION

1. Explain that you are going to look at our society as a whole. Who is out there? Who is my neighbor?

Have the group think of different groups of people in your community, such as blacks, the poor, prisoners, police, politicians, teachers, garbage men, alcoholics, divorcees, children, doctors, etc. Explain that if we are going to relate to people, we have to try and understand them and the problems they face.

Let the youth browse through newspapers to find groups of people in your community. Make a large chart on newsprint or blackboard. Take one group of people, and print the name at the top of the page. Make two columns beneath it.

What I can do personally	What the church can do

First, take a few minutes to discuss what you know about the group. What are their needs?

Then, brainstorm ideas for both categories: (a) what I can do personally, and (b) what the church can do. List.

Repeat this procedure for each group of people. Save all the newsprint sheets for future reference. The entire session can be spent on this exercise.

Ask: What is our responsibility as Christians with these people? (This question combines "what I can do personally" and "what the church can do.")

2. If you so choose, save time to work on a project, one with a message that says "We care!"

Suggestions:

(a) Make a slide show, using slides and an original script.

(b) Make collages, banners, posters, a mural, or a newspaper collage —on people.

(c) Make up role play situations.

(d) Find music and records which speak about people. Make a sound collage on tape.

(e) Film an interview, using a Kodak Ektasound 140, the "Talkie."

EVALUATION

1. Which session was most meaningful to you? Give everyone a chance to answer.

2. Which was your favorite activity?

3. What do you wish we had done differently?

4. Look at the purpose under each session. In what ways did we accomplish our purposes? In what ways did we not?

5. What projects or activities related to this mini-course should we continue to work on?

11

The Future of Me

Junior highs may not know what vocation they would like to pursue. However, most have some idea of the kind of future they want. At least, some are thinking about it. This is an excellent age to deal with "my future," for junior highs have a freshness and enthusiasm about life ahead. They have an idealism which should be shared and cultivated before it is squashed by "getting old." (You know, of course, that people over twenty are "old.")

Job. Marriage. Family. There is more to a future than those three. If your youth have done any of the values clarification exercises, they have experienced choosing priorities and deciding what is important to them. In this mini-course the junior highs will be doing "life planning." They will develop personal goals for their lives. Of course, what they plan now could completely change in five years. But, hopefully, this process will give them guidelines for determining priorities and for making decisions in the future.

SESSIONS IN BRIEF

I. In the first session, the youth will look at the "now" and the "future" to compare the concerns of each.

II. Marriage will be the topic of the second session. A married couple will be the resource persons and should discuss the important qualities in a marriage.

III. In the third and fourth sessions, the junior highs will do "life plan-
IV. ning." They will develop goals for their own future.

FOR YOU AND YOUR PLANNING GROUP

1. Study the entire mini-course. Discuss within the group any part that seems unclear.

2. Find a married couple who would be willing to talk openly about the questions listed in Session II. Check with your minister. He might recommend such a couple. Meet with that couple. Make sure they have a copy of the questions. Tell them the date, time, and place to meet with the junior highs.

SESSION I

Purpose: To compare my concerns of today with my concerns of tomorrow.

To examine the areas in which I will be making decisions (when and what kind of decisions).

PREPARATION

1. Go over the session. Make the list of categories to be used in part 1. List them on newsprint.

2. Gather materials
—posterboard for collage (22" × 28"); comes in a variety of colors
—lots of magazines and newspapers
—glue
—newsprint
—felt pens
—scissors

3. About the room—You'll need plenty of space for making collages, either floor or tables, or both.

THE SESSION

1. *Collage*

Have a newsprint sheet with the two lists of categories on display. The two headings should be:

Concerns Now	Concerns Later

Your planning group should have listed several categories under each:

Concerns Now	Concerns Later
School	College
Friends	Work–Vocation
Dating	Dating
Sports	Marriage
Getting along with parents	Raising a family

Ask the junior highs if there are any concerns not listed.

Direct them to the collage materials (magazines and newspapers). They are to make a collage which represents:

(a) what is important to them now.

(b) what will be important to them later. (Of course, they can't say for sure, but have them decide what they think will be important to them later.)

Suggest that they draw a line diagonally, or use a circular effect:

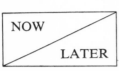

In whatever way they wish, have them make a separation between "Now" and "Later."

After everyone has finished, have them sit in a circle. Each should explain his collage.

2. Conversation: Virginia Reel Style

Have the group line up Virginia Reel Style—two lines of equal length, sitting on the floor, facing each other, about a foot apart:

o o o o o o o

o o o o o o o

There are twelve questions. The leader reads the first. The junior highs will have two or three minutes to converse with their partner about that question, each giving his answer. The leader will call time. Only one line moves to the left one person. The end person comes down and fills the empty space at the other end. Each person has a new conversation partner. The leader reads the next question. Again, each person talks with the person in front of him for two or three minutes. Time is called. The moving line moves again to the left, and so forth.

Remind the group that they are conversing. Keep talking. Use your own judgment as to the number of questions to use.

The following are conversation suggestions:

1. What would you change about your school, about the way you are being taught?
2. What makes your best friend your best friend? What is there about him that is special?
3. Do you think 14-year-old girls should be allowed to go on dates in a car? (You can change the age if you wish.)
4. What are the three things you most like to do?
5. Describe the best vacation you ever had.
6. If you had $500,000, what would you do with it?

7. What changes would you like to make in your church?
8. What's your opinion on ghosts?
9. Imagine yourself ten years from now. What will you be doing?
10. What do you think is the most important problem our country is facing?
11. What do you think is the biggest problem the church is facing?
12. What volunteer work could you see yourself doing in the future?

3. *Decisions*

Gather everyone together. Ask: What decisions do you see yourself facing in the future? Make a list on newsprint to keep for reference in the remaining sessions.

SESSION II

Purpose: To discover the various dynamics involved in marriage.

PREPARATION

1. Make sure the married couple knows when and where to meet. You should have given them the questions ahead. They will need time to think and to discuss the questions with each other.

2. The only materials needed would be the list made in part 3 of Session I. You may want to refer to it, especially if the list includes items dealing with marriage.

3. About the room—It should be a comfortable and informal setting. Meet in a home this session, if you can. The arrangement might look something like this:

THE SESSION

Begin the session by having everyone introduce himself in the following way:

>   Name
>   School
>   Favorite food
>   Favorite TV show

Explain to the group that you are going to interview Mr. and Mrs. —————— about their marriage. This is an open interview, so if anyone in the group would like to ask a question, he may. If a question is asked which neither of the couple wish to answer, he may pass that question.

Questions for the Interview:

1. How long have you been married?
   How many children do you have?
2. Recall what you wanted in a marriage partner when you were young. Did these criteria change as you got older? In what ways? What became more important to you as you approached marriage?
3. Is your husband/wife different from the type of person you thought you'd marry? How so?
4. What were the adjustments you had to make? You might list the adjustments year by year.
5. What happened when you had your first child? your second, etc.?
6. How did *you* change during different stages in your marriage? Describe.
7. They say that the problems one has during the first year are not the problems couples anticipate. First, what problems did you think you'd have during the first year? Were you right? Then, what were the problems that you didn't anticipate?
8. Could you tell us how you worked through a problem?
9. What do you see as the important qualities in a marriage? Describe.

SESSION III

Purpose: To begin planning for the future, deciding on goals and alternatives, and determining what is important in life.

PREPARATION

1. Go over the session. Make sure everyone in the planning group understands the life planning process.
2. Gather materials
   —newsprint
   —felt pens
   —plenty of paper and pencils

THE SESSION

1. *Counting the Cost*—an exercise for examining ways to accomplish a goal for the future.

(a) Pass out paper and pencils. Have each junior high decide on a goal, perhaps a career, or something he would like to accomplish during his lifetime.

Examples: I want to be a social worker
                    or an airline stewardess
              I want to write a book
                    to raise a horse
                    to do something for justice
    (b) Each person is to draw a chart like the following. (Illustrate on newsprint)

Positive	Negative

On this chart, he is to list those factors which will help him achieve his goal (positive side) and those factors which would be barriers to accomplishing his goal (negative side).

Example: Goal—I want to be a social worker

Positive	Negative
My strong desire to help people	Parents don't like the idea
Can go to college	I am lazy
Have good grades	Need money for education

Factors may be personal; they may deal with parents or friends; or they may be activities, sociological factors.

    Go around the circle, having each share his chart.

    (c) The next step is to concentrate on eliminating the negative factors. Have them take each negative factor and think of ways to eliminate the factor. Beneath the chart, have them list the suggestions for each.

Example: "Parents hate the idea."

    1. Go easy on parents. Don't argue.

    2. Provide them with data on types of social work, to show them it's not as dangerous as they think.

    3. Demonstrate a continuous interest.

Go around the circle, sharing these.

    (d) Now, for the positive side. Consider the positive factors and decide what things you will need to do to accomplish the goal (actions you could take). List these.

Example: 1. Look for volunteer work that I can do in the community.

        2. Try to get on the social action task force in my church.

        3. Find a college strong in social work.

Go around the circle, explaining these.

2. *Values in the Future*

Ask: What do you think will be of greatest importance to you at
        age 20
        age 25
        age 40
        age 68

Go around the circle for each age.

Have the junior highs put their names on their planning sheets. Collect them. They will be using them again in the next session.

SESSION IV

Purpose: Same as last session.

Last session you looked at one model for life planning, for testing a goal. In this session, the youth will try another.

PREPARATION

1. Go over this model with the planning group. Compare with last session's model. Which do they prefer? Why?

2. Prepare two newsprint sheets on the two models for life planning. Prepare another sheet on "Ways to . . ." (see exercise 1).

3. Have the chart on alternatives (exercise 1) mimeographed.

4. Gather materials
    —mimeographed sheets
    —newsprint
    —felt pens
    —paper and pencils, pens

THE SESSION

Display the first model for life planning (first newsprint)
Model I
    A. Set goal.
    B. Factors for achievement of goal
       Factors against achievement of goal

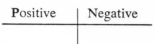

Positive	Negative

    C. Eliminate the negative factors.
    D. Take action on the positive ones.

Pass out their life planning sheets from the first session.

Display the second model for life planning, which they will use this session.

Model II

A. Set goal.

B. Think of all the possible alternatives for accomplishing the goal.

C. Rank each alternative according to your willingness to try it.

D. Self-contract—Actions to take

Examining Alternatives [1]

Display the following list of goals or "ways to." Feel free to add to the list.

1. Ways to make friends.
2. Ways to get along better with parents.
3. Ways to make faith more meaningful.
4. Ways of gaining more control over own life.
5. Things to do in leisure time.
6. Things to do to improve race relations in our school.

Divide into small groups of three or four persons each, who will work on the same problem. Ask one person which goal he would like to work on. Then, find two or three others who want to work on that problem. You have one group. Ask another person, and so forth.

Have them get together in their smaller groups. Pass out paper. Each group is to brainstorm as many alternative ways for working out the goal as they can, in about 5–8 minutes. The group works together to think of alternatives. Then, privately, each person is to rank the alternatives (1,2,3, etc.) according to his own willingness to try them in accomplishing the goal.

Bring everyone together. For each goal, have a reporter read the alternatives. Ask each person in the group to state his first three choices.

Have each person turn the paper over and make a list of his own goals—something he wants to do in life.

Pass out more sheets of paper. Suggest that they follow the same procedure, step by step:

(a) Pick a goal.

(b) Think of every kind of alternative possible that could accomplish that goal.

(c) Then, rank the alternatives.

Do as many goals as time permits.

Allow 5–10 minutes at the end for each person to write a self-contract concerning one or more of his goals. The self-contract is a statement of intent—what I will do—and a date by which it is to be done. Some terms in these contracts may refer to actions to be taken in the future. The dates may range from "by next week" to "by 19—."

EVALUATION

1. Which parts of this mini-course meant the most to you? (Go around the circle, so everyone has a chance to respond.)

2. Which part meant the least?

3. What reactions did you have to the married couple? Did you pick up any new ideas on qualities in marriage?

4. Which method for life planning do you prefer? Why?

5. What weaknesses do you find in these models? How might you do life planning differently?

12

In the Midst of Life: Death from a Christian Perspective[1]

Until recently you would not find a course on death in youth curriculum. Death is treated like sex was for so long: one should not talk about it openly. In Christian education death is discussed in the context of death and eternal life, resurrection, Jesus' victory over death. Indeed, that is a proper context, especially since our faith gives us a healthy attitude towards death.

But, our society does not celebrate death in the same way our Christian teaching suggests. In our world we see death in the context of war, crime, accidents, grief, and fear. Death brings to mind loss of loved ones, funeral parlors, and cemeteries.

We would like to avoid death as much as possible. Because junior highs are young, one might guess that they never think about death. Using value-related exercises, you could find that they do think about death. When asked to vote how many fear death, many will vote "yes." They have a great curiosity about the process of death. Many have seen people die. They wonder about funerals. They wonder what happens to the body.

The purpose of this mini-course is to introduce the subject of death to young people; to help them face the reality of death; and to give them an opportunity to consider the dynamics of death and dying in our society.

It should be noted that because of the very nature of the subject, the leader should be particularly sensitive to the needs of the group participants. The activities in this course are designed so as not to embarrass anyone. The youth are given opportunities to talk about their opinions and feelings, but are not in any way pressured. You will be pleased to know that leaders who have used this course have had very positive experiences. Youth are anxious to explore the subject and to discuss their ideas and feelings.

It is likely that initially some may feel uncomfortable at the thought of this course. Therefore, when suggesting the course, you will need to explain exactly what will be happening in each session.

SESSIONS IN BRIEF

   I. To introduce the mini-course.
      Questionnaire on death.
      Discussion of the questionnaire.
  II. Visit to a funeral home.
 III. Reactions to funeral home visit.
      Role play.
      Film (if available).
 IV. The funeral service—discussion of a letter written by a husband to his wife, indicating his wishes for burial, service, etc.
      A look at Biblical references to death.
      —Resource person may be used in discussion of the Biblical references.

FOR YOU AND YOUR PLANNING GROUP

1. Go over the entire course.

2. Make a list of questions to consider. Having youth on your planning group is a great help here. They will have questions you would have neglected.

3. Make arrangements with a funeral director for the visit (Session II). Most funeral homes are glad to have groups visit their facilities. Be sure to call several days ahead. Be prepared for a change in schedule if your visit is planned for a time of day when funerals are held.

4. You may want to use a film for Session III. Two suggestions are:

  a) "The Right to Die"—a sixty minute production of ABC News, first shown in January, 1974, on television.
     Available from: MacMillan Films, Inc.
                  34 MacQuesten Parkway, South
                  Mount Vernon, N. Y. 10550
  b) "Those Who Mourn"—a five minute film, which explores the death of a man and its meaning to his wife. The film suggests that the "comfort" promised in the original Beatitude may well lie in viewing the cycle of birth and death as a total reality.
     Write to: TeleKETICS
               Franciscan Communications Center
               1229 South Santee Street
               Los Angeles, California 90015

ALWAYS PREVIEW A FILM BEFORE USING IT.

5. If you plan to use a resource person in Session IV, make arrangements early.

SESSION I

Purpose: To introduce the subject of death to the junior highs.
To share opinions and feelings on the subject.

PREPARATION

1. Have questionnaire mimeographed.
2. Fill out the questionnaire yourself or with your planning group.
3. Gather materials
   —questionnaire
   —paper and pencils, if you choose to do the creative activity

THE SESSION

Most of this session will be spent discussing the questionnaire on death below. Since death is a rather uncomfortable subject for many, the more informal the atmosphere the better. Begin the session by explaining the purpose. Be very brief.

1. *The Questionnaire*

Distribute the questionnaire. Allow 10–15 minutes for its completion.

When everyone has finished, discuss the responses. You might start off by asking how many chose "a" for the first question, how many "b" and so on. Ask if anyone chose "e." Ask what other reaction he had to a study on death.

There may not be much discussion for questions 1 through 6, and No. 10, so concentrate on the others. For instance, on Question 7, "Death is discussed in my family . . . ," ask if anyone checked "a. openly." Ask that person (or persons) to describe situations in which death has been discussed.

Once the group gets used to giving a few of their opinions, the discussion should move along quite freely. You will probably find that junior highs have a variety of opinions and beliefs about afterlife and funerals. If someone wants to talk about an experience, let him.

During the discussion, questions may occur for which no one has an answer. Make sure to write these down.

QUESTIONNAIRE ON DEATH [2]

1. A study of death
   a. makes me uncomfortable
   b. is wrong
   c. is something I've really desired
   d. doesn't accomplish anything
   e. other _____

2. Have you ever seen an embalmed body?   Yes_____ No_____
3. Have you ever seen an unembalmed body?   Yes_____ No_____
4. Have you ever seen a person die?   Yes_____ No_____
5. When has a member of your family, a close relative, or a very close friend died?
   a. within past year
   b. within past two years
   c. within past five years
   d. over five years ago
   e. never
6. When did you last attend a funeral or memorial service?
   a. within past year
   b. within past two years
   c. within past five years
   d. over five years ago
   e. never
7. Death is discussed in my family
   a. openly
   b. with some discomfort
   c. only when necessary
   d. do not recall any discussion
8. What happens at death?
   a. person goes to heaven or hell
   b. just like dreamless sleep
   c. all mental and physical activity ends
   d. I have no idea
   e. other _____
9. Do you believe in some sort of life after death?
   a. yes   b. no   c. uncertain
10. Do you ever think about your own death?
    a. often   b. sometimes   c. occasionally   d. never
11. What does death mean to you?
    a. the end; the last process of life
    b. beginning of life after death, a transition to a new beginning
    c. joining of the spirit of a universal cosmic consciousness
    d. endless sleep, rest and peace
    e. other _____
12. What aspect of your death is most unpleasant for you?
    a. I could no longer have any experiences
    b. I am afraid of what might happen to my body after death
    c. I am uncertain of what would happen to me in an afterlife
    d. It would cause grief to relatives and friends
    e. All my plans and projects would end
    f. The process of dying might be painful
13. If you could choose, when would you die?
    a. in youth
    b. in prime of life
    c. just after prime of life
    d. in old age
14. What kind of death would you prefer?
    a. tragic and violent

    b. sudden, but not violent
    c. quiet and dignified
    d. death in line of duty
    e. death after great achievement
    f. suicide

15. If it were up to you, how would you like your body disposed of?
    a. burial   c. donation to science
    b. cremation   d. makes no difference

16. What kind of last rites do you desire?
    a. funeral with open casket
    b. funeral with closed casket
    c. funeral without body present
    d. memorial service
    e. I do not care

17. How have you felt about filling out this questionnaire?

2. Haiku and Cinquain (Optional)

If you have time and want to try a little creative expression, you could have the group make up HAIKU poems or CINQUAINS.

A haiku is a Japanese art form consisting of three lines. The first line consists of five syllables, the second of seven, and the third, five. The following are two examples of haiku on death:

    As life leaves I ask
    Will the everlasting arms
    Still be under me?

    Foam-padded casket
    Comforting the only one
    Who doesn't need it.

A cinquain is a French poetry form, consisting of five lines. Its composition follows these guidelines:

    Line 1: Title (a noun; one word)
    Line 2: Describes the title (two words)
    Line 3: Action words or phrase about the title (three words)
    Line 4: Describes a feeling about the title (four words)
    Line 5: Refers to the title (one word)

An example of a cinquain on death:

Death

Life's end

Ceasing to be

Fear of the unknown

Hope

3. Tell the group where to meet for the visit to the funeral home next session. Appoint someone to take notes or to bring a small tape recorder.

Ask the group which weeknight they could meet, in case the scheduled funeral home visit is cancelled.

SESSION II

Purpose: To see how death is dealt with in our society.

PREPARATION

1. Check on the funeral home the day before, and if necessary the day of, your visit. If you must reschedule, try to arrange the visit for the group's alternant choice.
2. Make sure you have arranged transportation.

THE SESSION

Allow at least an hour for the visit, not counting travel time.
What to expect:

The tour most likely will include the casket selection room, the chapel, and the embalming room. Some directors will show you the music facilities. If there is a grieving family at the home, the director will discreetly guide you around that particular room. You need not worry about intruding.

After the tour, the director should be available for questions. The youth will have plenty of questions. Someone should be making notes or taping this part of the session.

Note: After the session is over, it would be wise for you, the leader, to jot down some ideas for discussion next session.

SESSION III

Purpose: To share feelings and attitudes about the way death is dealt with in our society.
To confront the reality of death through role play.

PREPARATION

1. Make a list of questions from your notes to stimulate discussion.
2. If you have ordered a film for this session, make sure you preview it. Make a list of questions for discussion of the film.

THE SESSION

1. The first part of this session should be a discussion of the visit to the funeral home—negative and positive aspects. If discussion starts to drag, or if there are many who did not go on the tour, you might play the tape or have the reporter and those who did attend recall information.

Things to consider:
> the cost
> alternatives—burial
> > cremation
> > donation of body to science
> type of service

1. The Role Play

This role play takes little advance preparation. Select someone from the group ahead of time and explain privately what you are going to do and how you want him to help. This is important, or else the volunteer will feel left out of what follows.

Ask the volunteer to lie on a table, sofa, or floor as if he were a body in a casket. The other members of the group are asked to pass by the "deceased" and make some appropriate comment. Usually, there will be a lot of laughing at this time, which is all right.

Next, ask the group (except the volunteer) to sit in a circle in the middle of the room. Ask the volunteer to leave the room. Explain to the group that they are to imagine that "so and so" is really dead, that he is gone and never coming back. Point out the place where the volunteer was lying, so that all can see that he is gone. The tone which the leader sets at this point is crucial, since it is important for the group to take this part seriously. It is appropriate for the leader to speak for several minutes to set the mood, until all jokes and comments have subsided. Talk about the person, how much he was liked by all, things he did. Carry on for five minutes. Then, allow several minutes of silence for the group to reflect upon the loss of this person in their own lives.

After this silence, ask the group how they feel. Could they actually sense the loss of "so and so?" How close did they come to actually feeling the death of that person? Hopefully, the mood will be such that the youth may, to a certain extent, experience grief.

At this point, call the volunteer into the room. You might have given him a password cue at the beginning, so that he knows when to appear. This is RESURRECTION and may be a very joyful time for the group. They should be allowed time to express their joy by welcoming back the volunteer.

Note: Some groups will be more effusive in their expression of joy. Others won't be outward at all. That's all right. You don't want to be manipulative. If there is little expression of joy, go on anyway and ask if they did feel differently when the volunteer came back.

Ask the group to identify their feelings when "so and so" came back "from the dead." Discuss the whole experience. Was it effective? Could they "get into" the scene?

2. Film

If you have chosen to use a film, now is the time to view it. "Those Who Mourn" (five minutes) may not evoke discussion. It is a feeling-oriented film. It may be hard for the youth to describe their feelings after seeing it.

If you are showing "The Right to Die," hopefully you have a long enough session for viewing and discussion. You might have planned a longer meeting time for this session. Use questions you have developed from your previewing for discussion.

SESSION IV

Purpose: To examine Biblical references to death.
To evaluate funeral practices in light of the Christian faith.

PREPARATION

1. Mimeograph the letter "Dear Jackie" on pp. 171-172.
2. If you are using a resource person, explain the mini-course to him. Suggest that you need help in interpreting the various Biblical passages dealing with death, afterlife, resurrection, and the body at death.
3. Gather materials
   —copies of the letter
   —Bibles (*Good News for Modern Man*)

THE SESSION

1. You could begin by referring to the last session. Ask if anyone had any new thoughts on the role play. If there are those present who missed the last meeting, explain the role play.
2. Distribute copies of the letter "Dear Jackie." Explain that this is just one person's viewpoint and wishes. Have them read it and react to it.

Note: This letter usually provokes considerable discussion. One good way to discuss it is to take the letter a paragraph at a time and consider the ideas in each. Some people will agree with parts and disagree with others. You may not have strong feelings from everyone, because for many, this is the first time they have thought about some of these details.
3. What Do the Scriptures Say?

If you are having a resource person, both you and the resource person should lead this discussion.

Listed below are several passages which speak of death:
Psalm 23
Mark 8:35
John 14:1-7
Romans 8:38-39

I Corinthians 15:51–57
II Corinthians 4:11–12
II Corinthians 5:14–15
Galatians 2:20
Philippians 1:21

You may have others.

If you do not have a resource person, you might read aloud each passage—or, you could have each youth look up one and read it—and then discuss the implications of each.

> Try to rephrase it.
> What is the author trying to say? What is the main point?
> What is the view of death expressed?

This is a "group effort" Bible study. You all are working together to understand some difficult passages.

4. After consideration of the letter and the passages, ask the following questions:

> What does it mean to live a full life?
> Did Jesus live a full life?
> Do these passages say anything about the usual funeral procedures in our society? About the donation of our bodies to science?

FOR THOSE WHO HAVE EXTRA TIME OR MORE SESSIONS

1. Create a slide show on death. Write a script. Use original writing and/or poetry and Scripture passages. Find slides to coordinate with the script. Or, make your own slides (with acetate and borders, see p. 81). Or, take your own slides (with camera). You could use this production as part of a creative worship experience.

2. Develop several funeral and/or memorial services. Divide into groups, having each put together a service.

3. Man on the Street Interviews

Make up a list of questions for an opinion interview on death, funerals, etc. Arrange with a church school class (senior high or adults) to interview their class members some Sunday morning. Use tape recorders for the interviews.

EVALUATION

1. Did any of your attitudes or feelings toward death change because of this mini-course? Describe.

2. Which activities were the most meaningful? Which were the least?

3. What do you think we could have done differently to make this course more effective?

RESOURCES

Books:

Elisabeth Kübler-Ross, *On Death and Dying*. New York: The Macmillan Co., 1969.

Robert E. Neale, *The Art of Dying*. New York: Harper and Row, 1973.

Filmstrip:

Living With Dying—produced by Sunburst Communications
Available from:
MASS MEDIA
2116 N. Charles Street
Baltimore, Maryland 21218

Films:

"The Right to Die."

"Those Who Mourn." Both described on p. 163.

Dear Jackie:

For your help when I die, I want to set down on paper some of the things we have often discussed.

First when I die, call our minister and ask him to come where you are. He would be a visible reminder to you in those first hours that the love of God is present.

Then, telephone the funeral home. Call one in which the undertaker is a Christian. Tell the minister and the undertaker that I have died. Do not tell them that I have "gone home" or "passed away" or simply "passed" (which might recall many good bridge hours). Don't resort to the words that people use to dodge or evade the fact that death is death, that I will be dead. This may be a small point, but I believe the best way to deal with death is to accept it from beginning to end.

About the funeral. In one sense, the funeral makes very little difference because of our conviction that the body is not me. There wasn't some little butterfly soul inside me that fluttered away to be with God. All of me will have died. But, out of death we are sure that God will have taken me— the real me—unto Himself. So, the body is nothing. And yet, you will have a body on your hands.

You know we have talked over the possibility of donating my body to science. Since you are not quite comfortable with this idea and since I have not signed a commitment with the Medical University, go ahead and have the undertaker take care of my body. Also, I know that both our parents—if they are still around—would prefer some sort of funeral service.

However, I do not want a funeral service at a funeral parlor. I would like an interment service with just our families, followed by a memorial service at the church. So, tell the undertaker you want his services for embalming and interment. Tell the minister you want a small interment service and a memorial service. It seems most meaningful to me to have the graveside service signifying death and then move to the church where you'd be celebrating the resurrection, Christ's victory over death, and my resurrection. I realize it'll be hard to celebrate at such a time, but I think it'll have greater significance for you as times goes by. Both the graveside service and the memorial service should be expressions of praise to God. They should be experiences of worship. The minister will be able to give you suggestions for the service.

Now for details. . . . I do not like the idea of having my body for viewing. It seems somewhat idolatrous. After all, that body is no longer me and shouldn't be set up as if it were being worshiped. So, let's not gather at the funeral parlor at all.

Do not buy an expensive casket. Don't be pressured by any idea that you ought to honor me with a costly casket. No elaborate display of flowers. Perhaps you could suggest to people that instead of flowers, they might give a contribution to the church or the Heart or Cancer Fund; something like that.

For the memorial service. . . . Please don't have any solos, because emotion is so likely to be the only message of the singer. And please don't have the organist play any sorrowful music, like "Sweet Hour of Prayer." Ask that the organist play victorious music and play it at a good tempo; no dragging dirges. Perhaps he could play some familiar hymns. Do have the congregation sing "Lead On, O King Eternal," "O God, Our Help in Ages Past," or "Glorious Things of Thee Are Spoken."

Ask the minister to select Scripture passages of victory, like the last part of Romans 8. Include the Apostles' Creed, with the congregation participating.

Have prayers, primarily of thankfulness and praise. I am sure that the minister will include prayer for those who survive—that the Holy Spirit who is also called the Comforter will bring you peace, strength, courage; that the people may then live up to the principles—powerfully encouraging—of our faith.

No obituary, since it does not add to the worship of God. No poetry.

Take the children to the services, if they are as old as five or six. They too need to enter into the final service and know that something is really over, that it is all in God's hands, and that all is well. I am assuming that the air of victory will be so expressed that the children may feel it.

I truly believe that by the memorial service, my death can be one of our highest expressions of Christian witness. However I might have failed to communicate the Good News in life, it would make me very happy to know that my death succeeded in some measure to do just that.

13

We, the Church

It is amazing what junior highs, even those fresh out of communicant training, *don't* know about the church. They ARE the church and have a right to know what the elders and deacons do, what the mission of the church is, and why we worship the way we do. They need to know the meaning of baptism and communion, and what's involved in Christian education. Not only should they know, but a lot of them want to know.

Your first thought might be: "So I'm supposed to teach them all over again. And, what'll happen? They'll be asking the same questions next year." That could be true. But, this mini-course is designed to take you out of the "teacher" role. Instead of teaching them about the sacraments, you will be giving them an opportunity to clarify their own ideas and answer their own questions. Instead of telling them what the session does, let them *be* the session.

Junior highs don't usually feel a part of the church. More likely, they feel like "children of members," "the youth of our church," or "future members." It would be as unrealistic to delegate to junior highs all the responsibilities of adult church members as it would be to have them marry and raise families. But, the church is neglecting their contributions. As a junior high leader, you have an opportunity to show them that they are needed in the church. Their interest is likely to be higher at this age than at the senior high age. Help them find reasons to be involved in the church.

SESSIONS IN BRIEF

I. Session I takes a rather brief look at baptism and the Lord's Supper. Its purpose is to deal with questions that were not answered either in church school or communicant training.

II. Session II, on worship, includes an examination of the order of service. Each person will decide which parts are essential. They will develop alternative orders of worship.

III. In Session III and IV, the youth will assume the role of the session/
IV. church board of the church. In Session III they will deal with issues
  · concerning ministry within the congregation. In Session IV, they will decide on matters of service, the ministry of the church to the community.

FOR YOU AND YOUR PLANNING GROUP

1. Go over the session carefully. Jot down questions your planning group members have about baptism, communion, and the worship service. Refer to a bulletin.

2. You may need a resource person for Session I and/or Session II. Decide which, or both. Contact this person soon, to make sure he is available. A minister or D.C.E. would probably be your first choice. Your minister might recommend a lay person who could serve this function.

3. Plan to meet with the minister for an explanation of the duties of the session (or church board). Find out what the agenda is at present. He may give you a good agenda for the youth as they take the part of the session.

4. Ask a member of the session to meet with the youth for Session III and IV.

5. Find out all you can about what is happening in education in your church. This should be brought out in Session III.

6. Decide whether or not you can use the worship service to be created in Session II in an upcoming event.

SESSION I

Why is baptism so special? What does it mean to me personally? What about communion? What meaning does it have? These are some of the questions to be considered in this session.

PREPARATION

1. Go over the session carefully. What questions do the junior highs on the planning group have about baptism? about the Lord's Supper?

2. Gather materials
  —Bibles (*Good News for Modern Man*)
  —paper, pencils, pens
  —newsprint, felt pens
  —Book of Worship

THE SESSION

1. Pass around Bibles, paper, and pencils. Divide the group in half—one will work on the Lord's Supper, the other on baptism.

For Group I: Baptism

Have copies of the baptism service for the youth. In the P.C.U.S. it may be found in *The Book of Common Worship*, p. 47. The junior highs are to study the service and consider the following questions:

1. What promises of God are involved?
2. What promises do the parents make?
3. How is the congregation involved?
4. Note the elements in the service:
   —prayer
   —water
   —the Word
   —questions
   —the congregation

Have them rewrite the service of baptism. It should have all the essential elements. The wording of the prayers and the promises should bring out the meaning of baptism.

They could develop the entire service around the sacrament. How might they express to the congregation the significance of baptism? Scripture reference: Matthew 28:19–20.

For Group II: The Lord's Supper

Have this group look up the account of the first Lord's Supper in Matthew 26:26–30 and in 1 Corinthians 11:23–28. Questions to consider:

1. What happened at the first communion?
2. What elements were involved?
3. What is the significance of the broken bread and the poured wine?

Have each person think of a time when the Lord's Supper was most meaningful to him. Have each explain. Considering significant experiences of communion, the group is to create a communion service. Make sure all the essentials are in the service:

the Invitation
the Words of Institution
prayers
communion
the passing of the peace
music

The groups should have 30–45 minutes to work.

Call everyone together. Have Group I describe its service of baptism. Then, Group II explains its service of communion. Write down any questions and plan to find the answers.

2. Have the group sit in a circle. Go around, having each person complete this statement:

TO ME THE MOST SIGINFICANT THING
ABOUT BAPTISM IS . . .

Then, do the same procedure for:

THE LORD'S SUPPER IS IMPORTANT
TO ME BECAUSE . . .

Discussion may follow. Keep it free and informal.

SESSION II

What do all the parts of the worship service mean? What is worship? How might we worship differently?

PREPARATION

1. Go over the session with the planning group.
2. Check with the resource person, so he will know the time and place. You should have already explained that you want him to answer questions as to the meaning of the order of worship.
3. Secure several copies of the worship service bulletin.
4. Copy the parts of the order of service on a newsprint sheet.
5. Gather materials
—bulletins
—newsprint
—felt pen

THE SESSION

1. Display the order of service (on newsprint). Introduce the resource person. Have him explain the divisions and components of the worship service. Let the group ask questions at any time.

The resource person may stay or leave at this point.

2. Have the group examine the order of service and consider which parts they could leave out and have it still be worship for them.

Someone should start by saying: "I could do without. . . ." Draw a line through that part. Encourage others to do the same. Tell the group that if anyone disagrees and wants that part left in, he should speak out. If he receives enough support, then leave that part in. Continue until everyone is satisfied with what's left. You should have on the newsprint the *most important parts* of a worship service for the junior highs.

3. Keeping the important components in mind, have the group develop an order of service. (If you are having an event in the future for which you need a worship experience, here is a good chance to plan it.)

Decide on the theme for your worship, such as: Celebrating Life; Concern and Love for Others; Peace; Commitment; Joy; Community; Awareness; Wholeness; etc.

Divide into three or four groups, each group working on a particular part of the service. For example, one may work on confession and pardon or on prayers; one on music; one on the Word (proclamation through some medium—film, slides, art, story, dance).

This is THEIR service. Help them to make their own decisions about it.

SESSION III

Purpose: To take on the role of the session/church board of the church as it carries out the task of: MINISTRY WITHIN THE CONGREGATION.

PREPARATION

1. Arrange for a session member to be at your meeting.
2. Check with the minister to help you draw up a good working agenda. The agenda should include goal setting and tasks to implement the goals. The minister and session member should be able to tell you of present concerns of the session.
3. Gather materials
—newsprint
—felt pen

THE SESSION

Begin the session by telling the group: "You are the session of _____ Church. Tonight you will be looking at concerns and needs of the congregation. You will be setting goals and making plans for the rest of the year (or projecting plans for next year)."

Introduce the session member who will serve as a resource person. Have him explain his job as an elder. Encourage questions from the group. They will need to know what their responsibilities are if they are to serve as the session.

Have the session member list the needs at present (actual concerns of the church board). Put them on newsprint. Have the junior highs add more. For example, they may feel that a concern is that "church school is not effective."

Ask for a volunteer to moderate. The session member can explain his duties.

Write the Agenda on newsprint. Keep in mind the following process:
1. Concerns and needs
2. Goal setting
3. Ideas for implementing the goals—alternatives

4. Structure—program, actions for the year.

The junior highs may need help dreaming and goal setting. They will also need encouragement in devising concrete programs. Keep them moving, as they may get bogged down. Write out all plans on newsprint.

SESSION IV

Purpose: To continue in the role of the session/church board as it carries out its task of MINISTRY OUTSIDE THE CONGREGA-TION—SERVICE TO THE COMMUNITY.

PREPARATION

1. Arrange for the same session member or a different one to meet with the group. Explain that the concern is "service to the community." If he is new, ask him if he will share some of his feelings about being an elder.

2. Prepare an agenda.

3. Gather materials
—newsprint
—felt pen

THE SESSION

If you have a different elder visiting, introduce him. Have him share some of his feelings about being a session member. He should explain the concerns related to ministry outside the congregation. Put these concerns on newsprint. Let the group add to the list. They may point out needs in the community in which the church is not presently involved.

You can ask for another volunteer to serve as moderator. Using the same procedure as you did in Session III, carry on with the session meeting. Again, as leader, you will need to keep them from getting bogged down. Help them get their goals set and move on to implementation of programs.

EVALUATION

1. Were you able to get the feel of being a member of the session/ church board?

2. Did it help you to understand all that is involved in the ministry of the church?

3. What was difficult about this exercise? How might it have been done differently?

4. Do you have any different understanding of baptism or the Lord's Supper as a result of the first session?

5. What questions do you have about worship?

14

What Do We Believe?

In discussions with junior highs, it is surprising how often they bring up the subject of beliefs. Even though they may have been brought up in the church and taken communicant training, still they are asking: "What do we believe?"

A course on Christian beliefs would take an entire year and then some; you couldn't possibly answer all questions in a four-session mini-course. This could be one of the mini-courses you design yourself (see Chapter 18, p. 207). If you do, have the youth list all the questions they have about the Christian faith, about what they believe. You could then arrange the questions in categories. Have your planning group find resources to deal with the questions. You could use written resources and resource persons.

The most frequent questions junior highs raise relate to:

God
Jesus
the Trinity
Bible
Church
the future

This mini-course will explore questions about GOD, JESUS, THE BIBLE, and THE FUTURE. This course will give you an opportunity to learn together. There will be questions you can't answer. You and the group will need to do some digging—TOGETHER! It should be fun.

SESSIONS IN BRIEF

    I. In this session, the youth will explore various questions about God—who he is, his nature, his love, his relationship to man.

   II. In Session II, the youth will look at Jesus—who he was and is, the meaning of his life and teachings.

III. In this session, youth will look at the Bible as a whole, the total story. They will also consider its relevance for today and look at various experiences of Bible study.

IV. In the last session, the youth will compare their attitudes toward the future with Jesus' and the church's. What does hope mean? Also, they will explore ideas of resurrection, as it pertains to our daily living and to afterlife.

FOR YOU AND YOUR PLANNING GROUP

1. Go over the entire mini-course. You will need the junior highs' help on deciding which sessions to use. You may want to use all four and change some of the exercises to meet your needs. What questions do those on your planning group have about the Christian faith?

2. Decide if and when you want to use a resource person. The resource person would be there to help with questions. He need not lecture.

SESSION I

Purpose: To develop a statement of faith about God.

PREPARATION

1. Go over the session with your planning group. What questions do they have about God?

2. Study carefully the section on "God" in your denomination's statement of faith.

3. Contact the resource person, if you plan to have one.

4. Gather materials
   —Bibles (*Good News for Modern Man*)
   —paper, pencils
   —newsprint
   —felt pens
   —your denomination's statement of faith

THE SESSION

1. *God Is* . . .

On a newsprint sheet, write the words "God is . . ." at the top. Ask the group for answers to complete the statement. List.

2. *What Is God Like?—Luke 15:11–32*

Divide into groups of five or six each. Pass out Bibles, paper, and pencils. Have all the groups read Luke 15:11–32, the parable of the prodigal son, with one question in mind: What is the father like?

(a) List everything the father did.

Example: he had two sons
   he divided his property
   he saw his son, threw his arms around him, and kissed
      him
   he had servants put robe, ring, and shoes on him
   he had a feast

(b) How does the father treat his sons?

(c) If you were to say: "God is like this father," write a statement about what God is like. Have someone write the statement on a sheet of newsprint.

Call the groups together. Have each group share its statement on God. Display all the statements.

With all the newsprint sheets displayed, including the first one ("God is . . ."), ask: What questions do you have about God? List these on another sheet. See if you can find the answers in your denomination's statement of faith. The planning group might be able to help, if they have studied the statement in preparation.

Check the questions you cannot answer. Make arrangements to find the answers before the next session. Ask for volunteers to seek the answers. (You will probably need to call them during the week to remind them.)

Note: If you are having a resource person, you could use him here.

3. *A Statement of Faith about God*

From what you have learned about God (looking at all the newsprint sheets), form a group statement of faith about God. Write it out on newsprint. By the end of the four sessions, you will have a statement of faith by the junior highs, a declaration of their beliefs.

SESSION II

Purpose: To examine several images of Jesus Christ. To relate what Jesus Christ means to me. To develop a statement of faith about Christ.

PREPARATION

1. Go over the session carefully. List questions the planning group has about Jesus Christ.

2. Study carefully the section on Jesus Christ in your denomination's statement of faith. The planning group should be able to assist the entire group in searching for answers to their questions.

3. Contact a resource person, if you plan to use one.

4. Mimeograph the quote by Phillips Brooks (exercise 3).

5. Gather materials
   —mineographed sheets
   —Bibles (*Good News for Modern Man*)
   —paper and pencils
   —newsprint
   —felt pen
   —books with pictures of Christ, such as:
   > *Behold The Christ* by Roland Bainton (Harper & Row)
   > *The Faces of Jesus* by Frederick Buechner (Riverwood/Simon and Schuster)
   —books with quotes or poetry reflecting images of Christ, such as:
   > *Jesus: The Face of Man,* compiled by Louis M. Savary (Harper & Row)
   —slides or filmstrips on images of Christ
   > An excellent filmstrip is:
   > > THE GREAT MYSTIQUE SHATTERER, a production of:
   > > TeleKETICS
   > > Franciscan Communications Center
   > > 1229 South Santee Street
   > > Los Angeles, California 90015

THE SESSION

If you have found any pictures of Christ, have them visible to the junior highs as they are gathering.

1. Suggest that the group think of all the names attributed to Jesus Christ. List on newsprint. See how many of the following they suggest:

Lamb of God	Master
Son of God	King of Kings
Son of Man	Suffering Servant
Prince of Peace	Good Shepherd
Messiah	Light of the World
Savior	Emmanuel
King of the Jews	Redeemer
Teacher	Lord

2. On another sheet of newsprint, list all the responses to: What did Jesus teach and do? Make a chart:

Teachings	Actions

3. Pass out the mimeographed sheets of the Phillips Brooks' quote:

> Here is a man who was born in an obscure village, the child of a peasant woman. He grew up in another obscure village. He worked in a carpenter shop until he was thirty, and then for three years he was an itinerant teacher. He never wrote a book. He never held an office. He never owned a home. He never had a family. He never went to college. He never traveled two hundred miles from the place where he was born. He never did any of the things that usually accompany greatness. He had no credentials but himself.
>
> While still a young man, the tide of public opinion turned against him. His friends ran away. One of them denied him, another betrayed him into the hands of his enemies. He went through the mockery of a trial. And then outside of a great city of his day, he was nailed upon a cross between two thieves. While he was hanging there his executioners gambled for the only piece of property he had on earth—his seamless robe. When he was dead he was taken down from the cross and laid in a borrowed grave.
>
> Almost twenty centuries have come and gone, and today he is the centerpiece of the human race. All time dates from his birth. It is impossible to understand or interpret human history apart from the life of this one individual. It is well within our right to say that all the armies that ever marched, and all the navies that ever were built, and all the congresses that ever convened or all the parliaments that ever sat, and all the kings that ever reigned, put together, have not affected the life of man upon this earth as powerfully as has this one solitary life.
>
> —Phillips Brooks [1]

Have them read the quote in silence or follow along as you read. In reflecting upon this quote and the images of Christ you have been discovering, consider the statement: WHAT MEANS THE MOST TO ME ABOUT JESUS CHRIST IS. . . . Go around the circle, having each share his answer.

This exercise should initiate discussion about Jesus, his life, his teachings, and his relationship to us. Questions may be raised. Write them down. Look through your denomination's statement of faith for further understanding.

Note: The resource person would be helpful here.

4. Develop a group statement of faith regarding Jesus Christ (same as exercise 3 in Session I). Print this statement on newsprint.

OPTION

If you have access to the filmstrip, THE GREAT MYSTIQUE SHATTERER, or another filmstrip, you could use it in place of exercise 1. Have the group view the filmstrip and comment on those images which mean something to them. They will have preferences.

IF YOU HAVE EXTRA TIME

Make a slide production using the Phillips Brooks' quote as the script.

If you do not have slides, make some, using a visual maker and a Kodak Instamatic camera.

SESSION III

Purpose: To take a quick survey of the Bible.
To discover the purpose of the Bible, its importance and meaning for each of us.

PREPARATION

1. Go over the session with the planning group. What reactions do they have to Bible study? How relevant do they think the Bible is today? What questions do they have?

2. Make cards (at least 3″ × 5″) of the list of names in exercise 3, one name per card.

3. Go through the section on the Bible in your denomination's statement of faith.

4. Contact the resource person, if you plan to have one.

5. Gather materials
   —Bibles (RSV)
   —Cards for "Quickie Survey"
   —denominational statement of faith
   —newsprint
   —felt pen
   —masking tape

THE SESSION

1. Have a newsprint sheet on the wall, table, or floor, with the heading: "The purpose of the Bible is . . ." As the youth arrive, encourage them to write several ideas to complete that statement.

2. Gather in an informal setting (seated in a circle on the floor, or in chairs). Ask the group what kinds of experiences in Bible study have they had—both good and bad. Have them describe the best experiences. What made them good?

3. QUICKIE SURVEY

This exercise is a kind of game. Pass out the cards at random.
Names for cards:

God	civil war
created	Israel
Adam	Judah
fall	Elijah
covenant	Amos

Abraham	Hosea
Isaac	Jeremiah
Jacob	Babylon
Joseph	721 B.C.
Egypt	Exile
Moses	Isaiah
Exodus	Ezekiel
Sinai	Cyrus, the Persian
Ten Commandments	nationalistic
Joshua	Jesus Christ
Canaan	crucifixion
judges	resurrection
Samuel	Pentecost
Saul	persecuted
David	Paul
Solomon	Revelation

Each person should examine his cards and decide where chronologically his terms would be placed in a list referring to the Bible. First, have them arrange the cards they have in order. A lot of this will be guesswork. Pass around the masking tape. Each card will need a little roll, so that it will stick to the board (or wall).

In one chaotic mess, they should all approach a designated wall or blackboard and put all 42 terms in chronological order. This will take some time. It will be noisy. That's part of the fun.

After they have finished, ask if they are satisified. Are there any changes they'd like to make? Make the changes.

Now, the leader should slowly read the following story, filling in the blanks with the appropriate word as the youth have positioned it. When one is wrong, read it wrong, stop, and ask the group which one should go in that space. Make the change, and read on.

THE STORY:

"In the beginning, ___1___," is the beginning of the story of the Bible. It starts with God, who ___2___ the heavens and the earth. It was a perfect place, so He created man and woman, whom we have called ___3___ and Eve. But, man was not satisfied with what God had given him. He listened to the power of evil and rebelled against God. This we call the ___4___ of man. But, God did not give up on his creation. He made a ___5___ with ___6___ promising that He would not leave his people, that He would be their God. The covenant was carried on through ___7___, Abraham's son and through ___8___, Isaac's son. Because of ___9___, the Israelites moved to ___10___, and there were held in captivity until ___11___ led the greatest event found in the Old Testament, the ___12___.

On Mount ___13___, Moses received the ___14___. The Israelites became restless and turned to other gods. Finally, ___15___ brought the Israelites into the promised land, called ___16___. God appointed ___17___ to remind the people of their covenant with God. The Israelites wanted to be like other nations and have a king. So, the Lord had ___18___, the prophet anoint ___19___ Israel's first king.

And then came Israel's great king, ___20___. David's son, ___21___, built a beautiful temple for God (and an even bigger palace for himself). The kingdom became corrupt and judgment came in the form of ___22___. The nation split into ___23___ and ___24___.

God raised up prophets to preach his word. Those in the Northern Kingdom were ___25___, ___26___, and ___27___. But Israel would not repent and thus fell to the conqueror, Assyria. The prophet ___28___ warned Judah that she faced doom. The world conqueror, ___29___, brought down Judah in ___30___ and destroyed the temple. The Jewish people were led into ___31___. Two prophets, ___32___ and ___33___, preached of hope, that the glory of the Lord would be shown upon his people and a messiah would come.

The Israelites were allowed to return to Jerusalem when ___34___ conquered Babylon. The temple was rebuilt and all looked well for God's people. However, religion became too exclusive, too legalistic, too ___35___.. And so the time had come as foretold by the prophets, for God to show his love for man in the greatest possible way. He became man. ___36___ was born. His life and teachings told men about God's love. He called men to turn to God and to love others. His ultimate act was his ___37___, in which he took on the sins of everyone. He conquered death and evil by his ___38___. Many followers were baptized and received the Holy Spirit on a day called ___39___. His followers preached the resurrection and were ___40___.

A man named ___41___, who is responsible for many of the letters in the New Testament, encouraged the young churches to follow Jesus Christ. In the book called ___42___, we find the promises of God for the last days. And so, the Bible begins and ends with GOD.

Go back over the entire story. Try to clarify as much as you can. When questions arise which no one can answer, write them down and make plans to find answers.

SESSION IV

Purpose: To discover what we as Christians believe about the future, about resurrection, and about eternal life.

To examine the meaning of hope.

PREPARATION

1. Go over the session with the planning group. What questions do they have about the future, about resurrection, and about afterlife?

2. Go over the sections on hope, resurrection, and afterlife in your denomination's statement of faith.

3. Read the Scripture passages listed under part 2. What do they say about the future?

4. Prepare slips for each of the small groups. (See part 2 and the option section.)

5. Copy the section entitled "God Keeps His Promise and Gives Us Hope" on newsprint. See part 3.

6. You may want to have a resource person this session. The youth have probably heard a variety of things about "the last days." They will have questions about the book of Revelation which will stump everyone. Some may be familiar with books like *The Late Great Planet Earth* by Hal Lindsey, which correlates events in our world with Biblical signs.

There will no doubt be a lot of difficult questions. It could be a frustrating session, or it could be rather exciting. It can be exciting if they discover the more positive attitudes toward the future.

7. Gather materials
—Bibles (*Good News for Modern Man*)
—your denomination's statement of faith
—newsprint with two paragraphs (part 3)
—if using option, make copies of paragraphs for each small group (you could use newsprint)
—newsprint
—felt pens
—lots of paper, crayons, pencils

THE SESSION

1. A Picture of the Future

Pass out paper, pencils, and crayons. Tell the junior highs that they are to draw symbols of the future as they see it. Some symbols can refer to their own future and some to the world in the future. Some may refer to their ideas of the end of the world. And, some may deal with eternal life. Of course, they may use question marks or other symbols indicating lack of knowledge.

They have ten minutes to do this activity.

Gather together in a circle. Have each person explain his drawings. During this exercise, you should have newsprint set up so that you can list questions as they arise.

2. What the Scripture Says about the Future

Pass out Bibles (*Good News for Modern Man*). Divide into three groups and assign the following Scripture passages:
Group 1—Matthew 25:31–46

Group 2—2 Corinthians 5:16–21
   Romans 5:1–5
Group 3—Revelation 21:1–4

They are to rewrite the passage, trying not to use any of the same words. Pass out the respective slips with the following questions:

Group 1: Matthew 25:31–46
         What does it tell us about the future?
         What does it tell us about the way we should live now?
Group 2: 2 Corinthians 5:16–21
         What does it tell us about the resurrection life?
         What does it say about God's purpose?
         Romans 5:1–5
         What does it say about our future?
         What does it say about our lives now?
Group 3: Revelation 21:1–4
         What is the promise of the future?

Note: You may wish to use other Scripture passages. Some suggestions are:

Mark 8:31–38	1 Corinthians 15
Mark 13	1 Corinthians 15:51–57
John 3:16–21	Ephesians 1:11–14
John 12:20–36	1 Thessalonians 4:13—5:11
John 14:1–7	1 Peter 1:13–23
Romans 8:18–25	1 John 3:1–3
Romans 8:28–39	

3. Have the groups come together. Have each read its paraphrase. Discuss the questions. Make a list of questions which are raised and unanswered. Plan to seek help.

Display the following paragraphs: [2]

(1) God Keeps His Promises and Gives Us Hope

In the life, death, and resurrection of Jesus
God kept his promises.
All that we can ever hope for
was present in Christ.
But the work of God in Christ is not over.
God calls us to hope for more than we have yet seen.
The hope God gives us is ultimate confidence
that supports us when lesser hopes fail us.
In Christ God gives hope for a new heaven and earth,
certainty of victory over death,
assurance of mercy and judgment beyond death.
This hope gives us courage for the present struggle.

Ask: How does this statement compare with the passages? How do we define hope? What does hope mean to us as Christians? Discuss.

4. Develop a group statement of faith about the future, eternal life and the resurrection life we have now on earth.

Display all the group statements of faith drawn up in the other sessions. You should have a composite statement, WE BELIEVE THAT. . . .

OPTION

An examination of the following paragraphs may be used in place of the study of the Scripture passages (part 2). These paragraphs are taken from the third draft of "A Declaration of Faith." At the time this book was written, "A Declaration of Faith" was being studied by congregations in the Presbyterian Church in the United States. This proposed confession had not been accepted by the PCUS denomination. If accepted, it would become part of a book of confessions to be used in the PCUS churches. I offer it as an option because it is an attempt to explain beliefs about the Christian hope in simple language.

(2) All Things Will Be Renewed in Christ

In Christ God gave us a glimpse of the new creation
he has already begun and will surely finish.
We do not know when the final day will come.
In our time we see only broken and scattered signs
that the renewal of all things is under way.
We do not yet see the end of cruelty and suffering
in the world, the church, or our own lives.
But we see Jesus as Lord.
As he stands at the center of our history,
he will stand at its end.
He will judge all people and nations.
Evil will be condemned
and rooted out of God's good creation.
There will be no more tears or pain.
All things will be made new.
The fellowship of human beings with God and each other
will be perfected.
He will call all people and nations to account.
Evil will be rooted out of God's good creation.
There will be no more tears or pain.
All things will be made new.
The fellowship of human beings with God and each other
will be perfected.

(3) Death Will Be Destroyed

Death often seems to prove that life is not worth living,
that our best efforts and deepest affections go for nothing.
We do not yet see the end of death.
But Christ has been raised from the dead
transformed and yet in the same person.
In his resurrection is the promise of ours.

We are convinced the life God wills for each of us
is stronger than the death that destroys us.
The glory of that life exceeds our imagination
but we know we shall be with Christ.
We believe death is already a broken power
and that its ultimate defeat is certain.
Therefore in the face of death we celebrate life.
No life ends so tragically
that its meaning and value are destroyed.
Nothing, not even death, can separate us
from the love of God in Jesus Christ our Lord.

(4) God's Mercy and Judgment Awaits Us All

In the life, death, and resurrection of Jesus
God has already demonstrated his judging and saving work.
We are warned that rejecting God's love
and not caring for others whom God loves
results in eternal separation from him and them.
Yet we are also shown that God loves the whole world
and wills the salvation of all humankind in Christ.
We live by faith and not by sight,
in tension between God's warnings and promises.
Knowing the righteous judgment of God in Christ,
we urge all people to be reconciled to God,
not exempting ourselves from the warnings.
Constrained by God's love in Christ,
we have good hope for all people,
not exempting the most unlikely from the promises.
Judgment belongs to God and not to us.
We are confident that God's future for every person
will be both loving and just.

(5) Hope in God Sets Us to Work

The people of God have often misused God's promises
as excuses for doing nothing about present evils.
But in Christ the new world has already broken in
and the old can no longer be tolerated.
We know we cannot bring in God's kingdom.
But hope plunges us into the struggle
for victories over evil that are possible now
in the world, the church and our individual lives.
It gives us courage and energy
to contend against all opposition,
however invincible it may seem,
for the new world and the new humanity
that are surely coming.

Divide the groups into four smaller groups. Assign section (2) to one
group, section (3) to another, section (4) to the third group, and section
(5) to the last group.

Instruct the groups to rephrase their section. They are to rewrite it in such a manner that the other groups will understand the section from their report. Give each group their respective slip of questions:

For (2): What will happen to our world?

For (3): What does it say about death?
What does it say about life—life now?
How should we live?

For (4): What is the warning?
What does it say about those who might not be Christians?

For (5): What does it say about the way we are to live?

FOR OTHER DENOMINATIONS

Examine the part of your denomination's statement of faith concerning afterlife, resurrection, the Christian hope. See if you can divide it into three or four sections to be used in small groups. Write out questions for each section. A resource person could be helpful here. The language of many confessions is difficult for junior highs.

Reconvene the group and do parts three and four.

EVALUATION

1. Which of the four sessions were the most helpful? Why? Go around the circle, so that each may speak his opinion.

2. What should we have spent more time on?

3. How might we have dealt with the subjects differently?

15

In God We Trust: In Christ We Live

When I was twelve, I wanted more than anything else to live my life like Jesus would want me to. Then came communicants class. It was pretty poor. The minister was all right. But, we just didn't have enough time to cover everything. We did talk about what we believed and discussed the questions we'd be answering to join the church.

But, I wanted to know how to live the Christian life. Then . . . I don't know. . . . I got busy with school and everything and didn't think much about it.

Now that I'm 22, I'd really like to know . . . what does commitment mean? And, what about forgiveness? That seems so central to the Christian faith.

This is a familiar story. It's quite ironic—just when many young persons become full members of the church, they leave the church. Many junior highs have developed a strong personal faith. Often, it is a "between me and God" kind of faith. It isn't easy for junior highs to relate to other persons as Christians. Adolescence is giving them a hard time. They are fighting for their own identity. They want to be popular and do the things kids their age do. "Selflessness" and "forgiveness" are strangers in their world. But, many of them do understand that God loves them and wants them to love others in the same way.

So, how can we "get at" the Christian way of life, so it can become a reality. This mini-course examines four aspects—forgiveness, commitment, prayer, and self-giving.

SESSIONS IN BRIEF

I. In Session I, the youth will define forgiveness and check appropriate Biblical references. They will develop creative ways to forgive, including various types of the confession-pardon for worship.

II. In the second session, they will explore the following questions: To what are we committed? What actions would commitment require? What are barriers to commitment?

III. In Session III, the youth will examine types of prayer. They will create different acts of prayer.

IV. Self-giving. The youth will find ways to be self-giving. They will plan a worship service which will include some symbolic way to give oneself.

FOR YOU AND YOUR PLANNING GROUP

1. Study the entire mini-course carefully. Find out from the youth in your planning group just where kids are in relation to these factors of the Christian life. Ask them: To what extent can a junior high be forgiving? committed? self-giving?

2. Decide where and when the creative worship service (Session IV) could take place. Decide what groups will participate—youth? the entire congregation?

SESSION I

PURPOSE

To define forgiveness
To discover the Biblical meaning of forgiveness
To develop creative ways to forgive

PREPARATION

1. Study the session. Read over the passage: Matthew 18:23–35.

2. Check with the minister for samples of confessions and pardons used in worship services. The church secretary may have bulletins on file. See if you can borrow several.

3. Prepare newsprint with two quotes from the *Interpreter's Dictionary of the Bible*.

4. Gather materials
   —Bibles (*Good News for Modern Man*)
   —copies of bulletins, with confessions and pardons
   —newsprint
   —felt pen
   —paper, pencils

THE SESSION

1. *Forgiveness Is . . .*

Have a sheet of newsprint headed "Forgiveness is . . ." on the wall, table, or floor. As the junior highs arrive, show them the sheet and suggest that they write whatever comes to mind to complete the sentence.

2. *Parable of the Unforgiving Servant*

Divide into groups of five to eight persons each. Pass around the Bibles. Each group is to look up Matthew 18:23–35 and rewrite the story in a modern day setting. Appoint a reporter for each group. They have about fifteen minutes.

Call the groups together. Have the reporter from each group read their story.

3. *Quotes of Forgiveness from* The Interpreter's Dictionary of the Bible

Display the newsprint sheet with the following quotes:

> "Forgiveness appears here in the context of wholeness of life; to the paralytic, e.g., it meant recovery of ability to walk, to be fully a human being again."—p. 319.
> "Here it is seen as release from guilt, deliverance from anxiety and a burdened conscience, and recovery of peace with God."—p. 319.

What do these quotes say about forgiveness? Try to find parallels in present day situations where we can forgive others. Can a person help a person be whole? be fully human again? How? How might we help a person to be released from guilt or delivered from a burdened conscience? When someone does something bad to us, they may feel guilty. What can we do to show them forgiveness?

4. *Open-Ended Statements*

With everyone in a circle, use the following open-ended statements:
   a) A time I remember being forgiven was . . .
   b) A time I forgave someone was . . .
Have each person complete the statement and explain what it felt like (to be forgiven and to forgive someone). Was it a real experience of forgiveness, in light of what we have been saying about forgiveness?

5. *Forgiveness in Worship*

Have the group divide into the same smaller groups again. This time their task is to develop creative ways to forgive. Divide the worship service bulletins among the groups. Point out the confession and pardon section. Working with these confessions and pardons, each group is to consider symbolic actions or words of forgiveness which could be used in a worship service. They may write a new assurance of pardon or think up something using dance, art, music, dramatization, media, or some other creative form.

Give them as much time as possible, allowing ten minutes for them to share their pardons with the rest of the group.

Consider ways you might use these expressions of forgiveness. Perhaps you are planning a worship service in the near future.

SESSION II

Purpose: To discover to what or to whom we are committed
To consider levels of commitment
To find ways to act upon our commitment
To discover barriers to commitment

PREPARATION

1. Go over the session carefully. The youth in the planning group should be able to give you an idea of how junior highs feel about commitment. What keeps them from commitment?

2. Gather materials
—newsprint
—felt pen
—paper and envelopes
—pens, pencils

THE SESSION

Discussion is the basic method for this session. You should have a comfortable, informal setting. This session, in fact, this entire mini-course, is more effective with junior highs who have "become a group" (see Group Building, p. 61) who know each other pretty well. Otherwise, you may receive superficial answers; the session may run slowly and may not be very effective.

1. *To What? To Whom?*

Ask the group to think of all the things or people to which they are committed. "I am committed to. . . ." List all of these on newsprint. Then, ask them to think about their level of commitment. What does their commitment to each of these mean? Ask: How much time and energy do you give to each? Discuss each item on the list.

2. *To God, to Jesus, to Church?*

Commitment to God, to Jesus Christ, and to the Church may appear on the list. Some junior highs may be asking what the difference is. Give them an opportunity to express any confusion. Let them ask their questions. If there are any for which no one seems to have a satisfactory answer, make a note of the questions and seek out some answers before the next session.

When you get right down to it, commitment to God and to Jesus Christ involves exactly the same commitment. God sent his Son so that people would believe in God. Jesus pointed to his Father. The Church is the community of followers of Christ. To say you are committed to the Church means that you are among those followers who are committed to Jesus Christ, who is God Incarnate (God made man).

3. *What Does Commitment to God Mean?*

In what ways do you see yourself committed to Jesus Christ? to God? to the Church? List the junior highs' answers on newsprint.

Then, ask: In what ways do you wish you were committed? In other words, what actions would you take to indicate a deeper commitment? List.

4. *Barriers*

Ask: What keeps you from having that deeper commitment? What keeps you from doing those things which your commitment requires? List these on a clean sheet of newsprint.

Then, for each barrier, think of ways to get rid of it. What would you need to do to overcome that barrier to your commitment?

5. *Self-Contract*

Pass out paper, pencils or pens, and envelopes. The junior highs are to consider: How serious are you about commitment? Have them write a self-contract describing their commitment. Include what your commitment will involve. What actions will you take to act on your commitment?

Have them read over their self-contracts. If they are serious about them, they are to sign them. Then, put the contract in the envelope, seal it, and write their names on the front. They will be returned at the end of the fourth session.

SESSION III

Purpose: To identify different kinds of prayer

To look at the various aspects of prayer—when to pray, where, how

To pray creatively; to find creative expressions of prayer

PREPARATION

1. Go over the session. Discuss the kinds of questions junior highs would have about prayer.

2. Have planning group members gather books of prayers, expecially newer ones. Your minister of D.C.E. should have some. The following are suggestions:

> *Tune In,* edited by Herman C. Ahrens, Jr.
> *Lord, Be With,* by Herbert Brokering
> *Surprise Me, Jesus,* by Herbert Brokering
> *Prayers,* by Michael Quoist
> *A Kind of Praying,* by Rex Chapman
> *Are You Running With Me, Jesus?* by Malcolm Boyd
> *Good Lord, Where Are You?* by L. F. Brandt

3. Gather materials
   —books with prayers
   —several copies of a recent worship service
   —newsprint
   —felt pen
   —paper, pencils, crayons
   —clay

THE SESSION

1. Pass out copies of worship service bulletins. Have the junior highs look through them for types of prayers. List them on newsprint.
For example: Invocation
                Adoration
                the Lord's Prayer
                Confession
                Illumination
                Silent prayer
                Thanksgiving
                Supplication
                Intercession
                Offertory prayer
                Benediction
Go over each of the kinds of prayers. Ask the group for a description of each. If you get stuck on one and don't exactly know what it is, you could: a) have reference books there and look it up; or b) have a race. For the race, tell the group to find out the meaning when they get home. Search for it. Ask parents. Look it up. Call a church school teacher. When someone finds it, he is to call you, the leader. To keep from getting twenty-six phone calls, tell the person who called you first to call a couple of the other group members, who will then help him call others. So, everyone will know the answer has been found. This is one method for promoting enthusiasm in the group.

2. *Open-ended Statement*

Going around the room, have each person complete this statement:
    The type of prayer that means the most to me is . . . and why.

3. *When to Pray*

Ask the group to think of all the possible times when one might pray. List on newsprint.
Example: before meals
            in church
            bedtime

                    early morning
                    when in trouble
                    when very happy
Discuss which times different junior highs find appropriate.

4. Problems with Praying

Ask the group to think of problems or questions that they have about praying. List on newsprint.

Example: not knowing what to say
             not praying very often
             worry about being selfish

5. Group Work—Creative Prayers

Divide into small groups of five to six each.

a) Pass out the books of prayers. The groups are to spend 10–15 minutes browsing through the books of prayers. Pick out those that have meaning for you, those which perhaps express what you would say in a prayer. Make this an informal time, with the youth sharing what they found when they find it.

While they are doing this, a reporter in each group should be making notes on the reasons for liking certain prayers.

b) Each small group will *create*. They will decide on an act of prayer. Considering the reasons they listed for liking certain prayers, each group is to think of some new way to offer a prayer. It could be in the form of a dance, dramatization, song, art, or something written as a group.

They should have 15–20 minutes to work on this.

6. Call the groups together

a) Have the reporter tell the reasons for liking certain prayers. Share some of the favorite prayers.

b) Have someone from each group share their creative expression of prayer.

SESSION IV

Purpose: To discover ways I can actually give myself.

          To create a worship service which includes an act of self-giving.

PREPARATION

1. Read over the session. The question for the planning group to consider is: To what extent can junior highs be self-giving?

2. Make sure you have the creative confessions and prayers the junior highs developed in Sessions I and III.

3. Gather materials
   —newsprint
   —felt pens
   —clay, paper, slides, cameras, any other materials which could be
    used in planning a creative worship service

THE SESSION

1. *What Does It Mean to Give Oneself?*

Ask the group to think of as many ways as they can to give oneself. What
kinds of situations come to mind? What hints do you get from the Christian faith? How did Jesus give of himself? List ways on newsprint.

2. *Worship Service*

In Session I, the junior highs worked out creative ways to confess and forgive. In Session III, they created an act of prayer. Some of these could be incorporated into a worship service.

But first the junior highs need to come up with several creative acts of self-giving. To get started, you might refer to the offertory part of a worship service. In the first part of the offertory, the congregation gives its money to God's work. In the offertory prayer, the minister frequently prays: "We dedicate not only our material gifts, but also our very selves to your work on earth."

Divide into smaller groups. Each group should think of ways the offertory might be done differently, so that the congregation could offer themselves, instead of money. For example, the congregation could write a note about something they intend to do. They would indicate what time or talents they would be willing to give, or an action they might take in the week to come. They could put these notes in the offering plate. Or, the groups might think of some symbolic act to use in place of the collection.

After 15–20 minutes, call the groups together to share their ideas. Have the entire group decide which suggestions they'd like to use in an actual service.

Begin to work on a worship service. Incorporate the creative confessions and prayers. Use slides and other materials you have available. Plan to have this service in connection with a retreat or special service for the congregation.

You may not finish all the plans for the service. Save 10 minutes for part 3.

3. *Self-contracts*

Pass out the envelopes containing the self-contracts written in Session II. Have each person check his contract to see if what he intended included some form of self-giving. If it didn't, perhaps he would like to add to the contract. They may keep the contracts.

EVALUATION

1. Go over each purpose listed under each session. Discuss these. Which ones did you feel we accomplished? Which ones were not accomplished? Why not?

2. Which part of this mini-course was the most meaningful?

3. Were you free to express your own opinions and feelings? Did you feel comfortable in the group?

4. What questions do you still have about living as a Christian?

5. What do you think we should have done differently?

16

Those Who Encountered Jesus

What do we really know about Jesus Christ? What kind of person was he? Strong, mighty? How did he appear to those who knew him? Surely he did not appear strong and mighty as he hung on the cross, dying as a common criminal. King of the Jews? What mockery! Leader of his people? What kind of a leader is brought down so easily and displayed as a fool? Was it all a joke? Perhaps Jesus was just a gentle soul who never hurt anybody—kind of a weakly character. Weak? He had compassion for the poor. He defended the friendless. He forgave sins. He told of God's promise of new life. No man ever spoke like this!

> He was in the world,
> and the world was made through him,
> yet the world knew him not.
> He came to his own home,
> and his own people received him not.
> But to all who received him,
> who believed in his name,
> he gave power to become
> children of God.
>
> —John 1:10–12 (RSV)

Suppose you lived back then. Would you have been part of the world who "knew him not," or, would you have recognized him as the "One," the Messiah?

Knowing life as it is today and trying to picture life back then, it would be hard to imagine ourselves being confronted by Jesus. This mini-course offers the junior highs a glimpse of the past. They will be examining several individuals who encountered Jesus. With some imagination, perhaps they can experience through the character's eyes, what kind of a person Jesus was. As part of this exploration into the past, you will be asking: "How might I have met Jesus, had I lived way back then? What would he have said to me?"

SESSIONS IN BRIEF

The format for each session will be the same.

Session I
—Nicodemus (John 3:1–21)
—the Samaritan Woman (John 4:1–42)
—the Paralytic (John 5:1–18)

Session II
—the Adulteress (John 8:1–11)
—Lazarus (John 11:1–53)
—Zacchaeus (Luke 19:1–10)

Session III
—Rich Young Man (Mark 10:17–31)
—Mary and Martha (Luke 10:38–42)
—Blind Man (John 9:1–41)

Session IV
—Peter (Mark 8:27–33)
—Pilate (John 18:28—19:16)
—the Two Thieves (Luke 23:32–43)

FOR YOU AND YOUR PLANNING GROUP

1. Go over the basic format for this mini-course. Discuss the purpose:
To examine Jesus' relationships with people in various encounters in order to find out more about him. And, through an examination of who Jesus is, to find out the kind of life we are to live today.

To compare those encounters with similar situations in present day.

To consider what my reaction to Jesus might have been had I lived back then.

2. Check out the Scripture passages. Use *Good News for Modern Man*.

3. Gather materials for each session.
—plenty of newsprint
—felt pens
—Bibles
—*People of the Bible* by Cecil Northcott: Westminster Press, 1967.
—*Young Readers Dictionary of the Bible,* Abingdon Press, 1969.
(Secure more than one copy of the last two resources, if you can.)

BASIC FORMAT FOR ALL SESSIONS

1. Divide into three groups. Assign one "person who encountered Jesus" to each group. Their task is to come up with a profile on each person—as a detective would gather all the information he could about a suspect. Facts to find:
His character—what kind of person, rich or poor, nice, law-abiding citizen, criminal.

    Think of three adjectives to describe him/her.
His religious background—was he very religious, relatively, not at all?
What circumstances brought him to Jesus (or brought Jesus to him)?
What were his personal needs?
What was Jesus' response to him?
    What did he say?
    What did he do?

Print all these facts clearly on newsprint sheets. Make sure each group has access to the resources listed under "Gather materials." Allow thirty minutes for group work.

2. Call everyone together and have the first group display their newsprint. A representative should explain the facts to the entire group. Encourage questions and comments. Same procedure for Group II, and then, Group III.

3. With all three profiles displayed, ask: What does this tell us about Jesus, about who he was, and how he related to people? You are looking for more than one answer. List comments on a new sheet of newsprint. Have the group compare Jesus' responses in the three incidents. How would you describe Jesus?

4. Then ask: What parallels might we find in our world today? Ask them to make up a story of a similar encounter with Jesus, using a twentieth century person.

5. And finally, ask: Who of the three characters might you have been way back then? Go around the room, having each person answer.

When you get to this final question, have all the character profiles from the previous sessions displayed. In other words:

    in Session II, you'll be asking "Who of the six might you have been?"
    in Session III, "Who of the nine?"
    in Session IV, "Who of the twelve?"

It will be interesting to see if anyone identified with the same individual each week.

For Session IV: Expand that last question, "Who of the twelve," and ask the group to imagine what kind of circumstance (other than the twelve studied) might there have been way back then in which they would have met Jesus. Ask: What might he have said to you? Go around the room, each giving an answer.

EVALUATION

1. Could you get a clearer picture of Jesus Christ through this minicourse?

2. What did you think of doing your own research?

3. By examining the way Jesus related to people, what did you discover about the kind of life we are to live as Christians?

4. What do you think we should have done differently?

17

Other Religions

This mini-course is placed just before the section on "Creating Your Own." Actually, it should be a part of the chapter, "Creating Your Own," for you will have to do your own research. I am certainly not qualified to write a companion text on world religions for this course.

Junior highs have shown great interest in learning about other religions. A study on Judaism or Buddhism ranks highly in popularity. They are also interested in the differences in various Christian denominations. The guidelines suggested here could be used in explorations of the many denominations, as well as the major religions.

FOR YOU AND YOUR PLANNING GROUP

1. The planning group will no doubt have a job with this mini-course. This is a good opportunity to give them responsibility in choosing the creative activities and methods to use and in doing research.

If you can obtain the *Time-Life* kit THE WORLD'S GREAT RELIGIONS (described under "resources"), you and your planning group can examine it and decide the most effective ways to use it. Any book or resource on a major religion is going to be full of pretty "heavy material." The junior highs are your best resource for finding ways to communicate with junior highs. So, do plan this mini-course with your youth planning group.

2. Spend three to four sessions on one religion. There is no way to cover, say, Hinduism, in one night.

3. If you can find books and pamphlets, use them with the entire group. Have them look for the information listed below under "Guidelines for Research." Divide them into groups, each seeking different facts.

4. You could spend one or two sessions looking for facts. Have a resource person, a member of that religion, if possible, for a session. Spend one or two sessions on a creative activity dealing with the topic.

5. Give the group plenty of opportunities to discuss and to compare the subject to their own beliefs.

Six Major Religions: Christianity
                        Judaism
                        Hinduism
                        Buddhism
                        Confucianism/Taoism
                        Islam

GUIDELINES FOR RESEARCH

Find: 1. areas where practiced
       2. the basic beliefs
       3. the rituals
       4. the seasons and holidays, special events to commemorate
       5. famous leaders
       6. how culture relates to the religion
          how much effect the religion has on the culture
       7. kinds of music and sounds
       8. some art
       9. present day practice; where it is very popular
      10. if it is on the increase or decline

CREATIVE ACTIVITIES AND METHODS

1. Recreate a worship service or feast, one of the special events of the religion.
2. Make a series of posters or a mural describing the religion.
3. Put together a presentation especially for children, telling them about the religion.
4. Make your own slides and produce a slide show or filmstrip on the religion.
5. Consider a dramatic presentation.
6. Tape an interview with a member of the religion. If you can't find anyone, then do it as a role play interview. Tape it.
7. Put together a sound collage of the music and sounds of the religion.
8. As an arts and crafts activity, make some of the symbols. You could use a variety of materials: aluminum foil, clay, wire, paper.
9. Make a mobile of the symbols.
10. Make a banner which would carry symbols or an expression of the particular faith.
11. Write cinquains or haikus (see pp. 78 and 80), describing the religion or one of its beliefs.
12. Plan and make a presentation to a church school class (adult, youth, or children) on the religion.

RESOURCES

1. THE WORLD'S GREAT RELIGIONS is a kit available from
Time-Life Education
Rockefeller Center
New York, New York 10020
For each of the six major religions, the kit contains:
two filmstrips
two records
two cassettes
a teacher's guide (with discussion questions and filmstrip script)
a colorful educational reprint
four spirit masters (for duplicating)
bibliography
2. *Concern: World Religions*. This booklet is part of the CONCERN
discussion series, available from the Silver Burdett Company.

18

Creating Your Own

In this chapter, I am basically going to explain how I went about designing the mini-courses in the preceding section. As I worked on each, I saw numerous possibilities for expanding each into another mini-course. For example, in the course on Identity, there were so many options for sessions that it was hard to narrow it to four. All of the following relate to one's identity:

strengths and weaknesses

my past—family, growing up
living with parents
living with sisters and brothers
making decisions   The ones underlined were selected
problems with school   for "Identity," p. 136.
dating
peer group influence

worries and disappointments

conflicts

guilt
faith
moods (you could have four sessions on moods alone):
happiness
depression—feeling down
anger
resentment

You can create your own mini-courses. As I said at the very beginning, "YOU ARE FANTASTIC!" I believe you can do it. Now, all we have to do is get *you* to believe you can.

The following are guidelines for developing your own four session mini-courses:

1. Decide on a topic.
2. Think through purpose and objectives.
3. Outline possibilities for four sessions.
4. Decide on methods and creative activities (see those suggested in Section B.)
5. Get a youth planning group in on it. Their ideas are extremely helpful.
6. Write out your four sessions. Set the dates.
7. Gather your materials and resources.

1. Decide on a topic.

Where are you going to find the topic? Sometimes, you never get beyond this first step, for you feel like you have no idea what would interest junior highs.

(a) Keep a list of issues as they come to mind. Something you see in the newspaper. Something the junior highs mentioned—a question they may have raised. Look at junior high curricula. Your church has an education catalog. What kinds of subjects and issues do junior highs cover in church school? Talk to a junior high school teacher. They could tell you some areas you could explore with your youth. Every time you get an idea, write it down. This book should give you a few ideas. There are eleven topics explored through the mini-courses, and, as I have said, each of those could be expanded. See the long list of issues on p. 116. Surely, something there could be put on your list.

(b) Evaluate the needs of your group. This is not always easy. What *you* think their needs are can be quite different from their actual needs. The longer you have been with them the better. After four months, you will know a lot more than you did in the first few weeks.

Now would be a good time to jot down what you see as their needs. Next, devise some method to find out if you are right. How? First of all, you could compare your ideas with someone else who is working with junior highs—a church school teacher, perhaps. Then, use some values clarification techniques (see p. 70, p. 103 ff., p. 121 ff.) with the group. Open-ended sentences are valuable for this purpose, such as:

> I feel lonely when . . .
> The thing that really makes me mad is . . .
> People can hurt my feelings by . . .
> If I could change one thing about myself, I would . . .
> I have found that the best way to handle a problem is . . .
> I really need . . .
> My parents . . .
> I love people who . . .
> My worst problem is . . .
> The most important thing I could tell you about me is . . .

If the group has been together for a while, you can have each person complete the sentence in turn. If not, they could write down their answers on paper.

Talk with them about possibilities. Tell them you need their help in working out a four-session mini-course on a topic.

(c) IF YOU GET YOUR IDEA FROM A BOOK. There are several series of books written specifically for youth and for use in church school or youth group. One of these is the *Youth Forum Books,* published by the Thomas Nelson, Inc. Each book deals with a specific concern of youth and considers it in relation to the Christian faith. The following are a few of the titles:

Youth Considers Parents as People by Randolph C. Miller
Youth Considers Personal Moods by Reuel L. Howe
Youth Considers Doubt and Frustration by Paul L. Holmer
Youth Asks, Is God a Game? by Norman C. Habel
Let's Face Racism by Nathan Wright, Jr.
You Want to Change the World? So Change It! by Paul Simon

These are excellent books for youth to read and to discuss. There is a guide for leaders: *Creative Ways to Use Youth Forum Books.* If you have one of these books, and you feel it would be useful in your group, then you have your topic and one good resource book on that topic.

2. Think through the purpose and objectives.

What is your desired outcome? What would you like to see happen in your group? In the course on "Identity," I wanted to see our kids become aware of the fact that "It's good to be Me." I wanted them to discover their strengths. I was also concerned about peer pressure. My goal was that they weigh the influence of friends, keep it in perspective, and make their own decisions. And then, I knew that dealing with worry and disappointments was crucial for these youth. So another aim was that they develop a way to deal with worry and disappointments. Along the same lines, I wanted them to develop creative ways to deal with conflict.

Try to think of your goals in terms of action. You want them to do more than merely "understand" something. They do need to "understand" before they can "do." But, what would you like to see them DO? That's the goal!

IF YOU GET YOUR IDEA FROM A BOOK, read the entire book. What is the author's purpose? What is his hope for youth? Incorporate his goals into yours. Are they the same? If not, you will need to seek the opinions of a few other authors. (We will get to that in Step 7.)

3. Outline possibilities for four sessions.

"Four" is not a hard and fast rule. When I began working on the mini-courses, I expected some to be five or six sessions in length. However, for a couple of reasons, I kept them at four. First of all, if you are doing each session on a weekly basis, a month seems long enough to spend on one topic. I have found that during a six-session mini-course, I was beginning to lose people after the fourth. Now, I haven't made a controlled study of this problem, so I would be foolish to say that six sessions won't work. It really depends on your enthusiasm and the methods and activities you are using. There are situations in which you can maintain a high level of interest for a longer period of time.

Having all the mini-courses last four sessions provided continuity. The youth knew what to expect as far as time commitment was concerned. I would recommend expanding a mini-course for use in a conference or retreat setting.

As a leader, you must consider your topic and envision how you might break it down into four sessions. Identity was such a big one that I merely chose four areas I thought were relevant: strengths, peer group influence, worry and disappointments, and conflict.

In the mini-course on "Death," it was difficult to think of four areas of the subject, so the basis for the course was to cover the subject in four sessions. You may have to think of methods and activities as you consider the division. What activities might they do for each session?

Make an outline of the four sessions. For the mini-course, "Value Process," there are many possible values clarification exercises to use. For these I had about six different outlines. In fact, when I have used the "Value Process" course, I have done it differently with each youth group. You could make several outlines and decide which is best.

4. Decide on methods and creative activities.

If you have worked with youth for a while, you no doubt have a few ideas on which methods and activities work well with junior highs. Hopefully, you are constantly on the lookout for more. The more "goodies" you have collected, the easier it will be to design your own mini-course. Check out the ideas in chapter 6, pp. 61–98. Also, make note of the activities used in the eleven mini-courses in Section C.

Look over your outline for the four sessions, and consider which activities would be best for which sessions. The following suggestions may help.

(a) For the first session, you will want to introduce the course in an attractive way. Find out what the junior highs already know about the subject. Some of the values clarification exercises may be helpful. Sentence stems are appropriate for many subjects:

> Morality is . . .
> Commitment is . . .
> Injustice is . . .

Let the individuals complete the stems with their own opinions and feelings. You can make up "A Question of Priority" questions (see p. 105) on the subject.

You may want to spend part of the first session listing expectations. What do they want to get out of this mini-course? What questions do they have about the subject?

Discuss the purpose with them. It will be easier for them to get involved if they know the "why" behind their activities.

Plan to do some group building, if needed. Whatever the activities, try to create an atmosphere of openness and acceptance of each person. Show your enthusiasm for the subject. Use the positive approach. The junior highs will respond more enthusiastically if they get the impression the mini-course will be good. It's a far better approach than to start off by saying, "I'm not sure if this is going to work, but. . . ."

(b) Try to use a variety of activities. What could you do with drama? music? arts and crafts? audio-visuals? Would a presentation of some sort be appropriate? What resource persons could you use? Don't forget to keep lots of newsprint around. It is one of your most valuable visual aids.

(c) Be flexible. Some things won't work, but give it a good try. It is best not to quit too soon, for some junior highs will groan at anything you do. But, if you see that something really isn't working out, change it. You can be honest with the kids and need not feel embarrassed. Often, when an activity fails and nothing else is planned, the best thing is to substitute a discussion, a very free and informal discussion. Use open-ended statements on the subject. Give each person a chance to express his opinions and feelings. Group building is effective at times of failure. Surprisingly, when you fail, the youth seem more willing to support you.

(d) Plan to incorporate evaluation at several points. After the second or third session, you might ask for reactions to the activities. Your planning group can help you alter the remaining sessions.

Save ten minutes or more for evaluation at your last session. Make up some evaluation questions.

Suggestions for evaluation:

1. Did we accomplish our objectives?
2. Which activities or methods did you like the best? the least?
3. What could we have done differently? If you were to redesign this mini-course, what changes would you make?
4. Use the following sentence stems:
   "Because of this mini-course, I learned that . . ."
   "I realized that . . ."
5. Are there any changes in your personal opinions or actions as a result of this mini-course?

Evaluate with your planning group after the mini-course is finished.

5. Get a planning group in on it.

Ask a few kids to meet with you to discuss your outline. Their ideas are very helpful. It is nice having a youth planning group around to answer the familiar question: "I wonder if this would work with junior highs." As a team, work out the final outline for the sessions. Ask this group if they will be "responsible persons" (see p. 38) for this mini-course. Then, you can call on them for various needs: publicity, materials, enthusiasm, support.

Having a different planning group for each mini-course, project, or series of activities is an excellent way to involve a substantial number of junior highs. You will be giving them a sense of responsibility for their own youth group.

6. Write out your four sessions and set the dates.

Setting dates for mini-courses and other activities of the year's program is discussed in chapter 4 on planning (see p. 21). Even if you have completed your calendar for the year, there is always room for new ideas. Mention the mini-course to your group. Decide when it will take place.

7. Gather materials and hunt resources.

For most topics, you will probably need to do some searching. Look for materials—books, films, kits, magazines, slides, filmstrips. Check with your D.C.E. or whoever is responsible for ordering materials at your church. He should have catalogs.

IF YOU GET YOUR IDEA FROM A BOOK. In using books written for youth, like the *Youth Forum Books,* think carefully before ordering a dozen or so books. It would be great if each junior high could have a book and read it. But, with a youth group, I don't think many are going to take the time to do outside reading. Instead, *you* read the book. It will give you a good deal of information about your subject, with relatively easy reading. Then, look for other materials on the subject.

Write down several main points. Try to picture four sessions on the subjects, and then look for activities and methods.

DO NOT READ THE BOOK TO THE GROUP. Try not to use the book at all with the group. An exception: You could take a quote and have the youth react to it. If you do, remember to encourage more than one reaction. You could even make up open-ended statements relating to the quote. Go around the room, having each complete the statement.

Books do cause problems with creating your own mini-course. If you find a book on a subject you would like to use with your group, no doubt there is a lot of good information in it. You find yourself wanting to share it all. And, you can't. You don't want to drag on for ten sessions, one per chapter, so what do you do? It takes time, but you will have to narrow the subject. Pretend that you know a lot about the topic (actually, you got all your information from the one book). Now, you, the expert, are going to design a mini-course. Don't refer to the book. Just sit down and decide how you are going to handle your field of expertise. Write down a few notes, important points, possible divisions of the topic. From there, carry out your planning as described in the preceding pages.

The last step in "creating your own" is trying it out with some junior highs. That is the only way to find out which ideas actually work and which do not. There is nothing quite as exciting as seeing junior highs enthusiastically involved in something you have been planning.

A BRIEF EPILOGUE

Did I remember to tell you . . .

—that involving youth in planning and carrying out their own mini-courses, projects, and events takes time and patience. Using the planning group model, described in chapter 4, may not work every time you try it. Some youth will not take the responsibility as well as others. The important thing is not to give up on the model. You may be frustrated by it; and it may not work every time. But, do try it again. A new group working on a different program may make it all worthwhile. Even when it doesn't work, there is value in the fact that you interacted with the youth, that you were willing to take them seriously.

—to evaluate as you go along. You may see the need to make changes in your plans. And, evaluation lets you know how you are doing.

—not to get discouraged when it seems like nothing is working. There will be times when you will want to forget the whole thing. Get help; *don't let the church let you down.*

—that you may end up absolutely loving junior highs!

Notes

Chapter 3

1. Virginia L. Harbour, "A Platform for Youth Work," in *International Journal of Religious Education*, March, 1964.
2. Robert L. Browning, *Communicating with Junior Highs* (Nashville: Graded Press, 1968), pp. 24–25.

Chapter 6

1. Adapted from Sidney B. Simon, Leland W. Howe, and Howard Kirschenbaum, *Values Clarification: A Handbook of Practical Strategies for Teachers and Students* (New York: Hart Publishing Co., 1972), p. 174.
2. Lyman Coleman, *Serendipity* (Waco, Texas: Word, Inc., 1972), pp. 27–28.
3. Coleman, *Groups in Action* (Waco, Texas: Word, Inc., 1972), p. 26.
4. *Serendipity*, pp. 27–28.
5. Coleman, *Discovery* (Waco, Texas: Word, Inc., 1972), pp. 27–28.
6. Adapted from a Lyman Coleman exercise.
7. *Groups in Action*, p. 29.
8. *Ibid.*, p. 30.
9. *Ibid.*, p. 32.
10. *Ibid.*
11. Louis E. Raths, Merrill Harmin, and Sidney B. Simon, *Values and Teaching* (Columbus, Ohio: Charles E. Merrill, 1966), p. 30.
12. Adapted from *Values Clarification*, p. 36.
13. Coleman, *Breaking Free* (Waco, Texas: Word, Inc., 1971), p. 29.
14. *Ibid.*, pp. 26–27.
15. Helen and Larry Eisenberg, *The Omnibus of Fun* (New York: Association Press, 1956), p. 347.
16. *Breaking Free*, p. 27.

Chapter 7

1. *Values and Teaching*, p. 36.
2. Adapted from *Values Clarification*, p. 174.
3. *Ibid.*, pp. 58–81.
4. *Ibid.*, pp. 116–126.
5. *Ibid.*, pp. 38–55.
6. *Ibid.*, pp. 112–115.
7. *Ibid.*, pp. 228–231.
8. *Ibid.*, pp. 139–151.

9. *Ibid.*, pp. 250–251.
10. *Ibid.*, p. 36.
11. *Ibid.*, pp. 264–265.

Chapter 8

1. *Discovery*, pp. 27–28.
2. Adapted from *Values Clarification*, p. 112.

Chapter 9

1. *Serendipity*, pp. 27–28.
2. *Groups in Action*, p. 30.

Chapter 10

1. *Serendipity*, pp. 27–28.
2. *Groups in Action*, p. 30.
3. J. Wallace Hamilton, *Horns and Halos in Human Nature* (Old Tappan, N. J.: Fleming H. Revell Co., 1954), pp. 150–151.

Chapter 11

1. Adapted from *Values Clarification*, pp. 193–197.

Chapter 12

1. This mini-course was developed by Bill Williamson, Associate Minister of Westover Hills Presbyterian Church, Little Rock, Arkansas.
2. Several questions are adapted from a questionnaire in "You and Death" by Edwin S. Schneidman, in *Psychology Today*, June, 1971, p. 43.

Chapter 14

1. Adapted from an essay attributed to Phillips Brooks. Quoted in *Followers of the Way* (student's book) (St. Louis: Christian Board of Publication, 1970), p. 52.
2. "A Declaration of Faith," 3rd draft, P.C.U.S. (chapter 10). Quoted by permission.

24